# Navigating Loneliness

**TRIGGER**™
The mental health & wellbeing publisher

## ABOUT THE AUTHOR

Cheryl Rickman is a qualified Positive Psychology Practitioner and *Sunday Times* bestselling author and ghostwriter of twenty self-help, wellbeing and business books.

After her parents' lives were cut short, Cheryl decided to devote her life to helping others make the most of their own precious lives through the books she writes.

She specializes in writing practical books to help people fret less and flourish more, and is a Wellbeing Ambassador for the Network of Wellbeing.

Having qualified with a Certificate in Applied Positive Psychology in 2016, Cheryl also runs wellbeing retreats and delivers workshops on acceptance, balance and compassion, The ABC of Flourishing™.

Cheryl lives with her husband, daughter and two dogs in a country cottage in Hampshire, UK. She is an unashamed tree-hugger and nature-lover, has an overflowing bookshelf and her favourite colour is rainbow. She loves pizza and the seaside, but is not a fan of mushrooms or spiders.

You can find out more at www.CherylRickman.co.uk

# OTHER WELLBEING BOOKS BY THIS AUTHOR

*Be More Wonder Woman: Fearless Thinking from a Warrior Princess* (DK, 2020)

*The Flourish Colouring Book: Art Therapy Mindfulness* (CreateSpace, 2015)

*The Flourish Handbook: How to Achieve Happiness with Staying Power, Boost Your Well-Being, Enjoy Life More and Reach Your Potential* (CreateSpace, 2013)

*The Happiness Bible: An Ultimate Guide to Sustainable Wellbeing* (Godsfield Press, 2019)

*The Little Book of Resilience* (Gaia, 2019)

*The Little Book of Serenity* (Gaia, 2020)

*May You Be Well: Everyday Good Vibes for the Spiritual* (Pyramid, 2021)

*You Are Enough: Embrace Your Flaws and Be Happy Being You* (Summersdale, 2021)

# Navigating Loneliness

## How to Connect with Yourself and Others
## A Mental Health Handbook

Cheryl Rickman

# TRIGGER™
The mental health & wellbeing publisher

This edition published in 2023 by Trigger Publishing
An imprint of Shaw Callaghan Ltd

UK Office
The Stanley Building
7 Pancras Square
Kings Cross
London N1C 4AG

US Office
On Point Executive Center, Inc
3030 N Rocky Point Drive W
Suite 150
Tampa, FL 33607
www.triggerhub.org

A CIP catalogue record for this book is available upon request
from the British Library
ISBN: 978-1-83796-278-5
Ebook ISBN: 978-1-83796-279-2

Typeset by Lapiz Digital Services

Trigger Publishing encourages diversity and different viewpoints. However, all views,
thoughts and opinions expressed in this book are the author's own and are not
necessarily representative of us as an organization.

All material in this book is set out in good faith for general guidance and no liability
can be accepted for loss or expense incurred in following the information given. In
particular this book is not intended to replace expert medical or psychiatric advice.
It is intended for informational purposes only and for your own personal use and
guidance. It is not intended to act as a substitute for professional medical advice. The
author is not a medical practitioner nor a counsellor, and professional advice should
be sought if desired before embarking on any health-related programme.

To friendship – the kind others give me and the kind I have learned to give myself.

# FOREWORD

I am approaching my eighty-second year as I sit down to write this foreword. For the moment I am alone and therefore have the opportunity to look back across the years and reflect on a multitude of experiences. Friends tell me that I have had a most unusual life, and in some respects, I suppose, that is true. I have travelled to virtually every part of the world and lived in several countries.

Often I have been alone in dangerous and demanding situations where I have had to face acute danger and sometimes look death in the eye. Those experiences were nothing compared to the inner loneliness that I felt long before I became a hostage. The fear of being alone in a vast universe. That loneliness would so capture me that I would be lost in its embrace. Only those who have known that depth of loneliness will know what I mean. The loneliness that can propel you down a myriad of blind alleys in search of a solution.

Then came captivity. Five years as a hostage. Totally alone without the possibility of even seeing another person, let alone talking with them. I was frightened. Frightened that finally loneliness would overwhelm me and capture what remaining scraps of sanity I retained. Now it became a matter of survival. I had to deal with the problem otherwise it would deal with me and deliver a fatal blow.

It took me a long time to realize that the real key to dealing with the problem lies within. One has to look deep within one's inner being – with all its faults and contradictions – and learn to accept, and yes, even love oneself. It is not an easy process. No one can truly conduct an honest self-examination without realizing that there is a dark side to their nature. That is true for every human being.

Slowly, during those long years of isolation, I had to learn how to accept myself. I had to realize that I could not totally obliterate the negative side of my personality, but that I could work towards greater inner harmony and thus be more content within myself. This led to a releasing of creative forces that I never realized that I had. It also led to being able to convert loneliness into creative solitude. I realized that loneliness is a state of mind and could be dealt with.

It is my hope that this handbook will guide you towards that pathway.

**Terry Waite**
**November 2020**

# CONTENTS

# CONTENTS

# INTRODUCTION: YOU ARE NOT ALONE

There are people all around us. Everywhere. Eight billion of us co-exist on this planet. But that doesn't stop us from feeling lonely.

An estimated 9 million people in the UK, more than three in five Americans (61 per cent)[1], one in four Australians (25 per cent)[2] and 16.5 per cent of people over 15 in New Zealand[3] describe themselves as lonely. According to Our World in Data, between 25 and 48 per cent of people of all ages across many Western populations have reportedly felt left out, isolated or lacking companionship at some point in the past few years.[4] This figure rises to 50 per cent among disabled people.[5]

Such statistics provide evidence that, if you ever feel lonely, (rather ironically) you are not alone in feeling that way, whatever your social situation.

Millions of elderly people worldwide have been found to go at least five days a week without seeing or speaking to anyone, saying the television is their main source of company.[6] Yet loneliness is not only experienced by our elderly generation, with younger people reporting more lonely and isolated days than middle-aged adults, despite having larger social networks.[7] According to New Zealand General Social Survey 2018, loneliness in New Zealand adults is highest among youths aged 15–24.[8]

## Living Alone

Headlines about a 'loneliness epidemic' have been a regular feature in the media for some time now, mainly due to global demographics and health surveys reporting that approximately one quarter of all homes are now lived in by a single occupant. This figure has tripled since the 1940s, according to the US Census Bureau, with 40 per cent of city homes now single-occupancy – due, in part, to a rise in divorce, a decrease in people getting married and a rise in the number of people choosing to remain single.[9]

However, this rise does not mean loneliness is necessarily increasing. Living alone doesn't automatically mean you're lonely, just as being surrounded by people doesn't mean that you're not. Isolation can *contribute* to loneliness, but you don't have to be by yourself to feel lonely. Oftentimes, you can be surrounded by people yet feel lonelier than when you are physically alone. As such, living alone and spending time in solitude aren't accurate predictors of loneliness, nor do they confirm a lack of social support. People living alone may have many close and supportive relationships.

Equally, being in relationships and having an active social life doesn't immunize you from loneliness. Some relationships can deplete your energy while others can restore it. As such, when it comes to loneliness, it is the *quality* of connections we have which matters more than the *quantity*.

## Loneliness is Not Decreasing

The rise in single-person households isn't the only change. We tend to have less meaningful neighbourly connections than we did 50 years ago. And it is no longer the norm for 'villages' to raise children together. Yet, if a friend or relative moves to the other side of the world, rather than never see them again, as would most likely have been the case a few decades ago, advances in technology have facilitated a means of continued connection wherever we live in the world.

Additionally, while supportive labour unions, civic associations and post-war communities are less prevalent nowadays as a culture of individualism proliferates, there is no evidence to suggest people weren't just as lonely during the heyday of more connected neighbourhoods.

Whether loneliness is on the rise or not, one thing is certain: loneliness is definitely not decreasing. As such, it warrants our attention, our investigation and our intervention.

## Leaving Loneliness Behind

The good news is that while loneliness is unpleasant, it is resolvable, so you needn't *remain* lonely. Just as being alone needn't be a lonely experience. There is a way out of loneliness towards a life-less-lonely, one enriched with connection.

This book has been written as a warm hug for anyone who has ever experienced the painful feeling of loneliness, acting as a companion to guide you towards greater connection, both with yourself and with others.

### Social Isolation and Lockdown

In 2020, the Covid-19 crisis saw an unprecedented situation as virtually the whole world went into lockdown. Yet this was different to what people already experiencing loneliness faced, because this time we were self-isolating in unison, together.

Your individual experience will have differed from mine and others (a single mum stuck at home in a high-rise flat with three children would have a very different lockdown experience to a family of four with the countryside on their doorstep; who would have a different experience to someone self-isolating alone. Equally, those working from home had a different experience to those furloughed or made redundant). Yet, despite these diverse experiences, we were all in it together.

This cultivated a sense of solidarity. We were disconnected from each other, yet oddly, simultaneously more connected, given this shared requirement to stay home. We united to keep people safe, even though to do that we had to stay apart.

## About this Book

*Navigating Loneliness* is part of a Trigger Publishing series of books about managing mental health issues. Throughout this book you'll learn what actions you can take to tackle the main causes of loneliness and reduce it.

First, you'll be shown how to rethink loneliness and explore the benefits of solitude so that, once better connected with yourself and others, you can see it in a positive light and reap the benefits.

Next you will learn how to connect with yourself so you are able to enjoy and value your own company.

Finally, you will learn how to connect better with others so you can create at least one meaningful relationship with someone you can confide in.

In addition, there are several "compass points" which highlight especially useful or important information throughout, pointing you in the right direction, as it were.

At the end of the book you will find signposts to further resources should you need to seek further professional help.

My hope is that after reading this book you will be able to take what you've learned to become sufficiently supported and happy enough in your own company that being alone doesn't generate loneliness, rather that solitude is savoured and enjoyed as much as the increasingly meaningful connections you make with others.

# CHAPTER 1

# THE TRUTH ABOUT LONELINESS

## What is Loneliness?

Essentially, loneliness is a negative, unwelcome feeling of being starved of closeness to other humans, brought about by a lack of belonging, a lack of companionship and a lack of connection.

Unlike isolation, which is objective, as it is based on the number of social connections one has, loneliness is subjective: it's deeply personal and will depend on the individual experiencing it.

There are three main types[1] or 'dimensions'[2] of loneliness:

- **emotional or 'intimate' loneliness** (a lack of intimate and meaningful relationships and/or people to confide in)
- **social or 'relational' loneliness** (the relational lack of a trustworthy and supportive social network)
- **existential or 'collective' loneliness** (a feeling of collective detachment from others)

Each of these correspond to three main types of connection: **inner circle**, **middle circle** and **outer circle**, and each of these can go some way towards providing a defence against their corresponding type of loneliness.

- Our 'intimate' inner circle includes close relationships with between one and five people, which experts call our 'support clique'; they provide us with our main defence against 'emotional' loneliness.
- Our 'relational' middle circle of more casual friends provides a defence against 'social' loneliness, depending on the frequency of contact.
- And our 'collective' outer circle – a wider community of weaker ties – is our main defence against 'existential' loneliness.

In Chapter 6, 'Connecting with Others', we'll explore these different types of connection in greater detail and you'll be able to complete an exercise to help you figure out who fits into which circle and which type of connection warrants the most attention and action based on your own personal circumstances and experiences.

Loneliness can be **situational** and **transient**, meaning it can come and go or arise at specific times, such as over Christmas or at weekends, or can arise due to specific life circumstances, such as moving away from friends.

It can be **chronic** – a constant hum of discontent – or it can be **mild**, akin to an uncomfortable feeling of FOMO (Fear of Missing Out), where everyone else seems to have been invited to the party apart from you. Feeling left out can spark transient temporary lonely feelings, soon soothed once you feel included again.

Fundamentally, loneliness is the cognitive discrepancy between our desired and actual social contact; the difference between the quality of relationships we have and the quality of relationships we wish we had (and *need* to have so we may function well as humans, because connection helps us to function optimally).

> Fundamentally, loneliness is the cognitive discrepancy between our desired and actual social contact.

So, if we have the right connections and are sufficiently connected with ourselves, we are less likely to feel lonely, whether we are isolated or not.

## Loneliness vs Solitude

On one side of the street, a woman sits in her armchair knitting. She smiles to herself, remembering a fond memory. As she sits alone watching the blossom sway in the trees outside her window, she feels content. The phone rings. She pops the blanket she's knitting for her book club charity fundraiser onto her chair and answers the phone to a familiar friendly voice.

In the house opposite sits a young man. He's watching another episode of an exciting drama programme he wishes he could talk to other people about. They'd sip refreshing drinks and unpick the plot together. But he can't. He doesn't know anyone nearby. The television is the only company he's had in days. He scrolls through his phone, which only makes him feel more distant from the faces smiling smugly behind pixels of perfection.

Around the corner a man is counting down the days until he sees his children, whom he's only allowed to visit every other weekend since his divorce. His wife now has a new partner and their friends remained loyal to her rather than to him. He works hard and lives for the weekends when he can connect with his kids. The time in between is spent eating takeaways or ready meals and watching television. He can't seem to motivate himself to do much else. He's forgotten who he really is.

Two doors down, a woman sobs in the shower. She's just arrived home from her parents' house where she told them about her hopes for a new job, but they immediately turned the conversation back to their current woes. They never listen. Her daughter is away at university and her teenage son is gaming in his room, headset on, tuned out. She's going to wear her new top tonight, but her husband won't comment on it. He never does. He's too busy with work. She feels unseen and unheard. She'll feel the same tonight, despite being surrounded by friends. Nobody seems to see, hear or value her.

Each of these people is alone in these moments, but only three of them are lonely.

The first woman finds solitude soothing. She has a reasonably active social life, but cherishes the stillness of being alone, when she likes to knit, read and just think. Retired and living alone, she has a few dear close friends. She regularly attends clubs at the local village hall and volunteers for a local charity once a week.

The young man is starved of closeness. His scrolling on social media only makes him feel increasingly distant from the lives he views through his tiny screen. He doesn't know anyone in his street and hasn't made friends in his workplace since he moved away from his family over a year ago.

The middle-aged divorcee has lost motivation to get out and meet new people. He's too tired from work so he saves his energy for his children. The transition from married father to divorced dad has left him feeling bereft and lonely.

The second woman has a very active social, working and family life. She's overwhelmed and constantly surrounded by people. Yet she's never felt more alone.

As these examples demonstrate, there are a number of ways to feel lonely, and there's a significant difference between sweet spaces of solitude and painful moments of loneliness.

As poet and author May Sarton says: 'Loneliness is the poverty of self; solitude is the richness of self.' Or, as theologian Paul Tillich put it: 'Language has created the word 'loneliness' to express the pain of being alone. And it has created the word 'solitude' to express the glory of being alone.'

Whereas loneliness is about lack or loss, solitude is about space and solace. While solitude can be restorative and good for our health, chronic loneliness can be destructive and bad for our health.

You can *choose* alone time and savour solitude. Time and space to yourself can be a luxury, a delightful experience – but only if your innate need for connection and belonging has been met elsewhere.

And that is the key: if you feel adequately connected – be it to yourself or to others – solitude can be a positive experience, but only then. The key difference between loneliness and solitude, then, is this: unlike the allure of alone time, we never *choose* to be lonely. Conversely, many of us fear it. Indeed, according to the 2016 Viceland UK Census, young people are more afraid of loneliness than losing their home, job or physical health.[3] While in a US study carried out by social psychologists at the University of Virginia,[4] participants specified they'd rather endure a small electric shock than spend five minutes alone without their phone or another distraction.

Solitude – being alone – is often a choice. Loneliness never is.

Being alone can provide relief – an opportunity to pause in between the overwhelming pressures of daily life. Alternatively, the quiet can create a sense of foreboding – something to fear rather than favour. It all depends on whether you have the kind of social contacts you would like and whether you feel like you belong somewhere.

## Lack of Belonging

As Abraham Maslow's Hierarchy of Needs reveals, once our need for food and shelter has been met, our next most important in-built need is to belong.

Supportive relationships are vital to our wellbeing and sense of belonging; they give us an abundance of nourishment and make us feel as if we're a part of something. They offer guidance and encouragement, intimacy and closeness, allegiances and shared interests, safety and security, appreciation and worth, nurturance and reassurance, community and belonging, empathy and care.

No wonder we can feel so bereft without this.

That need to connect and belong is part of what makes us human – we're wired for it. We are social animals after all. As human beings, we've evolved to feel safest in groups. As such, belonging is at the very core of our existence.

Consequently, we need to feel seen, heard and understood. When we go unseen, unheard and misunderstood, we feel disconnected, disengaged and as if we don't belong.

With a sense of belonging we feel at home, accepted. Without it, we feel insecure, unaccepted, insignificant. And those are painful feelings.

Loneliness can also come from feeling as if we have nobody to confide in, from a lack of connection. To feel comfortable enough to confide, connections need to be strong and trustworthy and include a mutual sense of empathy.

---

Loneliness is about the absence of connection, rather than the absence of people.

---

## How Lonely Are You?
### The UCLA Loneliness Scale 2004

In 1978, Dr Daniel Russell developed a way to measure loneliness. Originally a 20-item survey, it has since been revised and shortened. This scale includes three questions measuring three dimensions of loneliness: relational connectedness, social connectedness and self-perceived isolation.

Circle which statement feels right for you for each question (hardly ever, sometimes or often).

| | | Hardly ever | Sometimes | Often |
|---|---|---|---|---|
| 1 | How often do you feel that you lack companionship? | 1 | 2 | 3 |
| 2 | How often do you feel left out? | 1 | 2 | 3 |
| 3 | How often do you feel isolated from others? | 1 | 2 | 3 |

Add up your scores for each question to give you a final score which will range from 3 to 9.

Researchers tend to group those who score from 3 to 5 as 'not lonely' and people who score from 6 to 9 as 'lonely'.[5]

If you score between 6 and 9 and are defined by this scale as lonely, consider why you feel lacking in companionship, left out and isolated. What has caused those feelings? Review the next few pages and ask yourself whether any of these causes apply to you and, if so, which ones specifically. We'll then explore what you can do about this with practical ways to tackle those causes.

## Causes of Loneliness

Remember, loneliness is common. Lack of belonging and connection are the main causes. When we dig deeper, however, there are various situational, mental, societal and technological causes of loneliness.

- **Situational:** Loneliness is often associated with transitions. Break-ups and bereavement, moving house and changing jobs can all cause loneliness. Single-parenthood, family estrangement and retirement can too. Poor health and disability can also restrict people from getting out and about to meet up with others.
- **Mental:** You might feel lonely because you've experienced rejection as a child from parents or peers. According to John Bowlby's attachment theory, loneliness can be linked to insecure attachment patterns and childhood rejection, which can generate distrust and hinder development of social skills. Consequently, chronic shyness or social anxiety can develop, making isolation preferable to interaction.[6]
- **Societal:** Wider changes in society have impacted loneliness. Rises in unemployment and working from home keeps people in their houses, disconnected from work colleagues. Meanwhile, churches, social clubs and other community gatherings have lower attendee numbers than ever before.
- **Technological:** Greater digital connection has created less human connection. Technological advances mean you can now perform more tasks with less interaction with other people – from shopping online to self-service checkouts where you don't even have to speak to a cashier. Paradoxically, larger social

networks and greater distraction caused by our mobile devices results in more time connecting virtually but less time having real life face-to-face connection with family and friends.

### Social or Unsocial Media?

Whether social media facilitates or debilitates connection depends on how it is used. If used to augment your offline contact network by forging new connections and enhancing existing ones, it can **reduce loneliness**, especially, according to researchers, if you are already highly social.[7]

Furthermore, social media can help introverts develop social skills and practice interaction from behind the safe barrier of the screen, but it shouldn't replace real face-to-face connection. In fact, if it's used to avoid in-person social interaction, it can 'displace time spent in offline social activities' and **increase loneliness**.[8]

Equally, when notifications interrupt real-life connections and distract from real-life conversations, it can generate disconnection. In fact, according to psychologists at the University of Pittsburgh, the more time spent on social media, the greater likelihood of feeling socially isolated.[9]

As such, social media has become somewhat of a paradox.

It can fuel 'compare and despair' – that illusory impression that everyone else is living better, more social and successful lives – which can increase envy and loneliness.[10] Yet, it can also provide greater opportunity to connect with like-minded people across the globe and provide access to resources to help combat the anxiety and depression generated by loneliness.

And, while friends on social media may offer encouragement, which can partially fulfil that human need to feel seen, heard and valued, if none of them pop round for a chat or message you, feelings of insecurity and insignificance can be heightened.

Meanwhile, an obligation to check in with everyone else, even while on your own, can reduce your capacity to connect with yourself. Constantly looking down at phones reduces our capacity to notice social cues or learn empathy – both vital components of genuine connection.

Whether social media enables or disables connection, research published in *The Journal for the Association of Psychological Science* shows the stronger your social skills, the more likely you'll benefit from social media,[11] whereas weaker social skills may cause feelings of inadequacy and isolation to arise as a result of social media usage.

This illustrates how it is not just an absence of *connection* which causes loneliness, but the absence of *tools* and *skills* to help foster connection, hence the importance of learning how to better connect (see Chapter 6).

# CHAPTER 2

# RETHINKING LONELINESS

## Isolation as Punishment

From an early age isolation is dished out as a punishment, so experiences of solitude are often negative. Off you toddle to the naughty step, to have 'time out' alone for bad behaviour, or to your room, banished to be by yourself to think about what you've done.

At school, this continues when children are sent out of class to sit alone or sent to isolation, excluded from working together with classmates. Solitary confinement is the ultimate punishment in prisons. No wonder there's a stigma surrounding solitude. Since childhood, we've been taught to associate alone time as bad time.

Meanwhile, togetherness is encouraged, as we're expected to move from our family tribe to school to work and on to having our own families. Making friends and meeting a mate are held up as the ultimate prizes in life and the only way to be truly fulfilled. And while relationships are important to wellbeing and survival of the human race, we are not taught the importance of positive solitude or how being alone can be good for our health.

We are not taught the empowering nature of solitude: that children who spend some time alone get the chance to learn self-reliance, to entertain themselves, to rise to challenges without always asking for help by default.

Perhaps it's time to reconsider how we see solitude, and reframe loneliness?

## Taboos Around Loneliness

According to the Campaign To End Loneliness, despite a fifth of Western populations self-reporting loneliness, almost two thirds of those people felt uncomfortable doing so.[1] So much loneliness remains unreported and hidden. As such, talking about loneliness is something we seem reluctant to do and yet, the more we talk about it, the more we see how common it is and the less taboo it becomes.

The negative connotation of the 'loner' label has contributed to this. A 'loner' is perceived as a social failure, a friendless introverted recluse who hides themselves away – either by choice, avoiding human contact, or as a result of society rejecting them. Being associated with this perception of being an outcast is not an attractive proposition.

So, to avoid the shame and embarrassment, we may not say we are lonely. This makes loneliness feel like it should be kept secret; something to 'admit' or 'confess'. So we say nothing and keep our feelings to ourselves. We don't want to be labelled as lonely but also, given how much we are wired to belong and how popularity is held in such high regard, being lonely feels like we are admitting to being unpopular, which feels like we've failed.

Yet loneliness has nothing to do with popularity, as we know that having a few good-quality connections is more important and has a more positive impact on our wellbeing than having lots of poorer-quality ones. Yet these fears and subsequent silence mean many miss out on all the available help and continue to feel lonely.

## Reframing Loneliness

Shame around loneliness comes from various places – from our fear of what it says about who we are if we are lonely and how that might impact how others perceive us, from our own insecurities and from societal labels of social failure. But what if we could shift how we viewed loneliness?

What if we taught our children about the great benefits of alone time and the great inventions and creations borne from time in solitude? What if we reframed the naughty step as 'reflection time' to disassociate isolation with punishment?

What if we talked about loneliness more openly? The more comfortable we become in doing so, the more we can remove the stigma by acknowledging that loneliness is just one part of the mental health conversation that we've begun to more willingly discuss.

And what if we changed *how* we talked about loneliness? Rather than 'admit' to feeling lonely or 'suffering' from loneliness and equating it to social failure, we could remind ourselves that loneliness is quite normal as a response to an unfulfilled human need, that there is nothing wrong with you if you feel lonely. Consequently, we could normalize loneliness, because we are all somewhere on the loneliness continuum.

What if we reframed loneliness as simply being a useful signal – alerting us to the fact that our connection gauge is empty and we need to take action to interact in order to fill it up?

## Loneliness as a Signal

As evolutionary scientists have been saying for years, loneliness, like hunger and thirst, has developed as an adaptive cue to drive us towards doing whatever is necessary to reproduce and survive as a species, to connect socially and intimately with each other.

Tribes, families and couples have historically given us the mutual protection and help we need in order to survive. We have always banded and bonded together. In an evolutionary context, disconnection becomes life-threatening, as early humans were heavily disadvantaged when they were isolated from their tribe. This has led loneliness to evolve as a warning sign; a call to action to reconnect and thus survive.

Viewing loneliness from this evolutionary perspective can shift things.

We don't feel shameful when we say, 'I'm hungry' or 'I'm thirsty', but we might when we say, 'I'm lonely'. Yet, loneliness, like hunger and thirst, is simply a feeling that flags up that we are deficient in the nutrients of connection.

In this way we can reframe loneliness as a helpful warning sign, which can then guide us into taking the tiny steps toward what we need for our survival, towards connection. We can then see loneliness not as something to be ashamed of or embarrassed about, but as an evolutionary prod, guiding us towards finding something that is missing.

## How Being Alone Makes You Feel

*'I have to be alone very often. I'd be quite happy if I spent from Saturday night until Monday morning alone in my apartment. That's how I refuel.'*
Audrey Hepburn

You might find your energy depleted by others yet revitalized after some time alone, or maybe the converse is true and you feel energized when socially engaged and depleted after time spent by yourself. You may even experience both, depending on who you're with and how much energy you have. There are many variants involved in determining how time alone makes you feel.

While your upbringing and genetics are partially responsible for your temperament and how aloneness impacts you, so are the levels of dopamine you naturally have stimulating your neocortex – the part of your brain responsible for logical thought and language.

Dopamine is a feel-good chemical. If you naturally have low levels of dopamine, you may feel under-stimulated and become bored easily, so you may seek out social interaction to feel good. Conversely, if you have high levels of dopamine, you may find extra stimulation overwhelming and seek to avoid it, opting instead to enjoy the peace and quiet of solitude.

But hormones are only part of the story; we all interpret aloneness differently, depending on our age, personality, dependence level and lifestyle.

It's worth assessing how being alone makes *you* feel and why that might be so. For example:

- Do you need the constant comfort of company to escape from depression, anxiety or low self-esteem?
- Do you seek out company because you're too troubled by your thoughts when you're alone for too long or devoid of that safety net of validation?
- Does being alone make you feel uncomfortable and anxious, rather than relaxed and nourished?
- Does being alone make you feel unworthy and abandoned rather than joyful and free? Or do you find sweet serenity in enjoying time to yourself to do what you like, with less restriction and more freedom?

- Does being without a significant other to navigate parties or visit restaurants with make you feel uncomfortable about being alone? Might this be related to societal expectations and your fears around what others might think?

Knowing how being alone makes you feel and why is an important first step to navigating your way forward.

*Duration* of aloneness also matters.

You might feel fairly comfortable being alone, just not for too long. A few evenings alone might be bearable – enjoyable even – but any more may feel like too much and trigger loneliness. Perhaps that's where you need to focus your attention – on finding the right balance. Or maybe you only need a good chat on the phone on a regular basis, without feeling the need for in-person connection, but when nobody phones you feel yourself spiralling into loneliness. If so, could you schedule in a regular call with someone you enjoy talking to?

You could be someone who needs regular social connection and try to get out to the pub or gym most days because that constant company and conversation comforts and engages you. As such, you might have become dependent on that level of regular connection and feel bereft when by yourself.

Alternatively, you might feel happy being alone as long as you have some firm commitments in the diary – such as a monthly brunch date or evening in with close friends – and as long as regular WhatsApp messages are forthcoming. Perhaps it's only when the calendar is clear and your messages are being ignored that you start to feel isolated and lonely.

Consider how *you* feel if you go a few days without seeing or speaking to anyone. Does too much social contact feel overwhelming to you? Or does too little negatively affect your mood? What level of contact feels right for you? What might feel like the right balance between sufficient connection and adequate alone time? Or does the thought of any time alone make you feel vulnerable to negative emotions?

Answering these questions can help you establish the right balance between connection and alone time as you schedule time to do what matters most to you (we'll explore this more in Chapter 4 about self-connection).

> *'Solitude is independence.'*
> *Hermann Hesse*

How you feel about being alone can also depend on your level of dependence. If you're an independent person, you will likely feel better about being on your own than a more reliant person, who is dependent on help. If you are prone to helping others, you may *need* to feel needed, which leads to feeling surplus to requirements and empty when there's nobody else around. Whereas, if you are constantly surrounded by other people, escaping from those demands might appeal, but perhaps you'd still rather have some companionship on a deeper level?

Depending on your mindset, your personality and your preferences, solitude can therefore be a place to escape to or escape from.

### *Honjok:* The Tribe of the Alone

In some cultures, solitude has become a positive lifestyle trend. In South Korea, where there are now more single-person households than those containing families, those prioritizing individualism have their own hashtag and name: '*Honjok*', an amalgamation of the words '*hon*' (alone) and '*jok*' (tribe).

*Honjok* individuals choose to live a life where solitude is sought-after and celebrated rather than fought against and rejected. And the culture of *Honjok* is growing so rapidly that restaurants and event organizers are now allocating more single-seat tables.

The *Honjok* are part of a growing global phenomenon driven by an increasing number of people opting to stay single, with the *Honjok* lifestyle emerging as an antidote to and relief from the constant contact that comes from living in such a highly populated and fast-paced world.

*Honjoks* have the freedom to choose where they go and what they do without having to consider other peoples' needs, wishes or dietary requirements. When you're on your own, you can do whatever you like. By living in this way and favouring self-fulfilment, *Honjoks* are rejecting societal expectations and pressures around marriage, family and work, choosing to live their own lives without compromise.

As the *Honjok* demonstrate, while connection and engagement are good for us, disconnection and disengagement can be too.

There are now more single-person households in South Korea than those containing families.

## Shifting Perceptions

Thankfully, you have more control over your response to being alone than you may realize. And, even when solitude has been an enforced and wholly negative experience (for example, if you have been abandoned, left behind or have needed to escape a toxic relationship to find yourself alone), by exploring ways that solitude can nourish and energize you, and through improving your connection with yourself and others, it's possible to shift how you feel when you're alone.

Rather than fight loneliness, you can accept it and deal with it by filling it with thoughts, ideas and plans; you can populate the space with productivity and love; and you can reframe it as solitude once you get to know its benefits. We'll explore all the ways solitude can become a welcome retreat rather than something to fear in Chapter 3.

Albert Einstein once remarked, 'I live in that solitude which is painful in youth, but delicious in the years of maturity.'

It can take a lot of work to feel this way about solitude. As Terry Waite, who spent five years in isolation after being taken hostage during the 1980s, told me: 'To become more at ease with yourself and your own company and to get accustomed to being alone can take time.'

'It took me a long time to get adjusted to it in captivity,' says Terry. 'But, having spent five years there alone, I'm much more accustomed to it now and I've learnt how to manage it... It isn't easy at first, especially if you've been used to being associated with others, but it's a rewarding road towards enjoying your own company.'

Every journey starts with a single step, so – let us begin.

# CHAPTER 3

# APPRECIATING ALONE TIME AND CELEBRATING SOLITUDE

*'I wish I could show you, when you are lonely or in darkness, the astonishing light of your own being.'*
Hafiz

*'You don't need to be a monk to find solitude, nor do you need to be a hermit to enjoy it.'*
Leo Babauta

## Seeing Solitude As An Opportunity

Imagine if, rather than feeling empty, invisible and insignificant when you're alone, you felt good, energized and fulfilled.

Solitude gives you the chance to feel that way because it offers the opportunity to work on yourself. It provides freedom, time and space away from the hustle and bustle to contemplate and cultivate the life you want, to reflect and create and learn. As such, alone time needn't be negative. The positive power of solitude comes from the realization that solitude isn't being *by* yourself; it's being *with* yourself.

---

The positive power of solitude comes from the realization that solitude isn't being *by* yourself; it's being *with* yourself.

---

When we see solitude through a lens of escaping from the masses, as a place of retreat and renewal, we can more readily celebrate and appreciate the time we get to spend alone, rather than fear and avoid it.

As American essayist Alice Koller writes in *Stations of Solitude*: 'Being solitary is being alone well... luxuriously immersed in doings of your own choice, aware of the fullness of your own presence rather than of the absence of others. Because solitude is an achievement.'[1]

However, it takes time to move from feeling lonely when you're alone to enjoying the solace of solitude. So let's take a look at some of the benefits that spending time on your own can offer.

*'And all I loved, I loved alone.'*
*Edgar Allan Poe*

## The Benefits of Positive Solitude

Solitude offers:

1. Freedom to do as you please
2. Connection with the present
3. Freedom to be your true and authentic self
4. Connection with yourself
5. Space to navigate the negative and gain perspective
6. Space to dream and plan
7. Enhanced creativity

*'I love to be alone. I never found the companion that was so companionable as solitude.'*
*Henry David Thoreau*

## 1. Freedom To Do As You Please

There's an appealing sense of freedom when nobody is making demands on your time or attention. When you're not beholden to anyone else, you get to fully control how you spend your time and do as you please, uninterrupted. That may sound selfish, but when much of your life may be spent putting other people first, it's refreshing (and necessary) to take time to care for yourself.

You can't pour from an empty cup, and the better you look after yourself, the better you can take care of others when the need arises. As such, it's always worth investing time in doing what fills your cup and makes you feel good.

Being by yourself offers an interlude, an opportunity for rest and renewal. With no obligation to talk to anyone or do anything you're not keen on, you can unwind and recharge your batteries.

---

### EXERCISE: Choose How to Nourish Yourself

It's not uncommon to spend time alone numbing ourselves rather than nourishing ourselves – bingeing on Netflix or scrolling through social media feeds, for example. But these activities do not always serve our best interests. So, it makes sense to consider which activities truly nourish and refuel you. Which self-care rituals fill up your cup?

- Make two lists. In the first list, write down self-care rituals and enjoyable activities that you love to do. If you had a day off to do anything you liked and had to choose restorative activities that made you feel good, what would you choose to spend your time doing? For example, you might love to take a long soak in a bubble bath, to dance round the kitchen to your favourite music or to sit in your favourite chair, drinking a cup of your favourite tea while reading a good book. Or perhaps you'd prefer to take a walk in nature, go for a refreshing swim or paint with watercolours. The only rule for this list is that the activities should nourish, relax or energize you, rather than numb or deplete you (so no scrolling through social media, watching TV/movies or comfort eating or drinking).

- On the second list, consider what sparks your interest. What would you love to learn or improve? List activities that would help you to grow as a person, such as watching inspirational TED Talks or listening to audiobooks on your topic of interest. Alternatively, you might wish to learn to play an instrument, try out a new recipe or plant a window box herb garden.

- Select seven of these nourishing activities, ideally four or five from the first list and a couple from the second list, and write them down on a Post-it note or piece of card. (If you have too many, save some for a new list another time. If you don't have enough, write down what you have and keep a notepad by your bed in case you think of more.)

- Stick the Post-it or card on your bathroom mirror or fridge, or anywhere you will see it regularly.

- Whenever you have some time alone which is free time, spend it on one of the activities on your list. As a result, you'll begin to habitually devote your alone time to doing things that light you up and help you grow, so you may flourish.

## 2. Connection with the Present

Moments are what make up our lives, yet we are often too busy or distracted by other people to really focus on the ones happening in the present, in the *here* and the *now*. When you're alone, you can consciously pay more attention to what you are doing and to the world around you. For example, it's much easier to savour the experience of eating a delicious meal or strolling through a woodland without someone talking to you.

Sometimes, however, when it comes to feeling connected to the present moment, we can get in our own way. Instead of being mindful (the art of paying attention to the present moment), we tend to dwell on what we've said or done in the past, or worry about what might happen in the future. We're either ruminating on past regrets or anxiously planning ahead, all of which disconnects us from the present and prevents us from enjoying each moment and staying grounded.

On top of that, our lives, like our minds, are busy – brimming with demands and the constant pressure of never-ending to-do lists. We either sleepwalk through our routines on autopilot, not noticing our now, or we rush around from one task to the other, with no time to savour each moment.

Mindfulness is easier to practice when you're on your own, so solitude not only offers us the chance to focus and work through our to-do lists more effectively, without distraction, but, as a result of this productivity, it also provides more time and space to pause and reconnect with life – with your now.

What's more, the stillness of solitude sharpens your senses, so you can notice details you might otherwise have ignored, appreciate the ordinary moments and find joy in the smaller things that would ordinarily get lost in the din – the leaves swirling in the courtyard, the patterns of sunlight dancing across the wall, the cat thoroughly washing its paws.

As well as being a useful tool to reduce anxiety and manage stress, mindfulness helps us feel better connected to ourselves and our surroundings. When you're on your own, you can more readily tune into your bodily rhythms and notice how your body feels at any given moment. This gives you greater clarity about when you ought to eat, nap, sleep and create.

Mindfulness also enables you to more readily tune in to the rhythm of the Universe, to feel part of and connected to something bigger than yourself.

Connecting with your natural surroundings provides both a mental and a physical balm. Indeed, woodland walks have been proven to reduce blood pressure, heart rate and production of cortisol (sometimes called the 'stress hormone') – hence the popularity of the Japanese art of forest bathing across the globe.

The natural world itself can, in the absence of human interaction, also assume the role of companion – one which never lets us down, never interrupts us and is always there to sit peacefully with, marvel in awe at and boost our wellbeing. This is comforting, especially if you're dealing with life changes yourself, because the changing seasons can remind us that everything moves on, that change is natural, that 'this too shall pass'; this loneliness shall pass.

Nature walks can now be prescribed by doctors globally as part of a social prescribing initiative to help with mental health and wellbeing.

---

### EXERCISE: Sensory Awareness

This sensory exercise will help to bring you back to the present moment. It can be done sitting down and observing the world around you, or while walking through a natural setting.

- First, look around you at your surroundings. In your head, list five things you can **see** in this moment.
- Next identify four things you can **hear**, such as the sound of birdsong or traffic in the rain.
- Now list three things you can touch or **feel**, like the clothes against your skin, the wind in your hair or the solid wood chair you're sitting on.
- Now choose two things you can **smell**, like cut grass or fabric softener.
- Lastly, pick one thing you can **taste**, even if it's just this morning's toothpaste or toast.

This tool uses each of the five senses to help you tune into your own sensory awareness of the present moment. It also uses counting as a cognitive tool to move you from using the emotional side of your brain to the logical side, interrupting thought patterns and bringing you back to the now.

Once you've finished this exercise, pause for a moment to consider how much more connected you feel to your surroundings, to your body and to the present moment. You can practice sensory awareness whenever you feel disconnected from your 'now', and the more you do it, the better you'll get at it.

## 3. Freedom to be Yourself

Being by yourself gives you the chance to *be* yourself. When there is nobody else around, you don't need to pretend. You get to just be *you*.

Solitude can give you the freedom to be authentically you without having to wear a brave-faced smile and cover up your true feelings, without having to pander to expectations or change who you are to fit in.

Being away from outside influences gives you the chance to find your own voice, to step away from group-think so you can tune in to hear what you truly believe and want to say or stand for. In this way, solitude can help you to hone and shape your own view of the world, to develop a clear perspective untainted by external influences.

This is especially critical in a world of 'shoulds', which can often fuel feelings of inadequacy. We can all feel this 'not good enough-ness' to varying degrees, the shackles of 'should' which tell us we should be better, thinner, prettier, smarter, younger, friendlier. When you're alone, you have the freedom to accept yourself without anyone else looking at or judging you.

This can be incredibly liberating, especially if you've escaped a toxic situation and are alone as a result. If you've chosen aloneness over toxicity, the freedom to be who you are is a critical part of the healing process. How many people stay stuck in toxic relationships for fear of being alone? If only they knew the positive benefits that solitude can offer on their journey.

Hiding who you truly are only serves to amplify disconnection from others, whereas the more time you spend just being yourself by yourself and getting comfortable as you are, the easier it becomes to share that true self with the world.

Spending time alone gives you the chance to assess your strengths and values, so that you can live in alignment with them.

The values you hold dear and your unique strengths form the fundamental essence of who you are and what you care about. They spell out your 'why' and give your life meaning. And when your daily life is aligned with your values and you use your strengths, it's easier to present your authentic self to the world with confidence. For example, if you value integrity and one of your unique strengths is courage and you find yourself getting triggered when you're surrounded by people at work who bend the rules to suit themselves, you might combine your strength and values and be brave enough to find a new job where colleagues value integrity as much as you do. Or if you value fairness and equality and one of your character strengths is a love of learning, taking a course on diversity in the workplace and speaking out about it would authentically combine your values and your strengths.

Your character strengths are different from your skills, talent or spark; they are the collection of traits which form your individual nature, the hallmark of your character that guides your thoughts and actions. For example, being organized or a good communicator are skills, being proficient at painting is a talent and the fact that you enjoy painting is your spark or passion. Whereas creativity, curiosity, honesty, perseverance, kindness and humility are all character strengths.

Aristotle believed that the more we act in accordance with our character, the better people we become. So it's really worth spending time alone to help uncover what these hallmarks are, so you can have greater confidence in being who you are when you're in company.

---

### EXERCISE: Uncover Your Unique Signature Strengths and Values

Over decades of study, two of the founding fathers of Positive Psychology, Professor Martin Seligman and Dr Neal Mayerson, created a methodology to rank 24 human signature strengths. The resulting scientifically validated 'VIA (Values in Action) Inventory of Strengths' survey is a free online test featuring 120 questions that provides incredibly accurate results about what our own individual signature strengths are, ranked in order.

- Visit www.viacharacter.org to take the survey and find out what your top five strengths are. These might range from 'hope', 'loyalty' and 'humour' to 'leadership', 'creativity' and 'zest'.
- Write your top five strengths down in a notebook or journal, or you could even get creative and write them out in calligraphy or paint them on a piece of card to put on your wall.

- Now you know what your signature strengths are, try to notice when you are using them. At the end of each day this week, reflect on this and write down where and how you used your top strengths. In a Chinese education study,[2] this exercise was found to boost life satisfaction.
- Additionally, you could write an affirmation about your top one or two strengths. For example, 'I am creative. I am open to trying new ways of doing things,' or 'I am hopeful. I expect good things to happen in the future and work to make this likely.' Put it somewhere you'll be able to read it often, either out loud or in your head.

Your values are shaped by what matters most to you. They provide you with an inner compass to guide your day-to-day decisions and a lens through which you see and show up in the world most authentically. The following questions will help you to assess your values. Although they are 'big picture' and you won't necessarily answer them in one go (and your answers may also change over time), they will show you which values are most noteworthy right now.

- **Which values are most important to you?** What values would you/do you teach your children? What values do you want your life to reflect? (For example, you might value kindness, equality, cleanliness, hard work, honesty or humility, etc.) Why are they so important to you? Consider whether you've chosen them based on your ingrained family or cultural teachings, or whether they are deeply truthful to you personally. The latter are the values that matter most in being true to yourself.

- **What is uniquely significant to *you*?** Being a good parent/sibling/friend perhaps? Treating others as you wish to be treated? Taking care of people? Speaking up for others? What could you do more of in order to live those values? Perhaps you could pause before responding to family members? Or join a campaign group to support a campaign that matters to you?
- **What do you sometimes feel pressured into doing or being? List your 'shoulds'.** For example, 'I feel like I *should* wear smart clothes in dark colours to look professional, but I prefer to wear casual, brightly coloured clothing.' Or 'I feel like I *should* tone down my personality to be accepted.' Write down ways you could start to abide by your *own* preferences and personal choices and bring out your own unique personality, rather than do what you think you *should* be doing. Then go ahead and slowly but surely bring your whole self out into the open. For example, if you wear dark clothes because you feel like you 'should', you could start by putting on a bright scarf or piece of jewellery.

When your actions flow from your values, you can be true to yourself, but it's easy to lose sight of your core values. Your answers to these questions will renew your insight into what matters most to you. Based on your findings, you can create your own personal inner compass, a gentle reminder which can be used to guide your everyday actions. This will enable you to say 'yes' or 'no', depending on what matters most to you, and to show up more readily as your true self, rather than showing up as you think you 'should' based on external sources.

## 4. Connection with Yourself

Spending time alone gives you the chance to not only *be* who you are, but to gain a deeper understanding of who that actually is, to get to know yourself better. Understanding your strengths and values is a great starting point, but getting to know what you want and need is different.

When you're surrounded by others, they will often need something from you. Time alone gives you the chance to consider what *you* want and need in your life in order to thrive, and what gets in the way of that. Solitude allows you to explore what you treasure, what triggers you, what sparks joy in you, and what doesn't. It's the perfect opportunity to ponder on what is and isn't working in your life, to uncover truths and find clarity. You can find within you all the answers you need, collect your thoughts and make sense of things.

As you tune in to your own internal insight about who you are as an individual, you can become increasingly comfortable and confident in your own skin. This is because alone time gives you the chance to better understand what you're good at.

When I spoke to Terry Waite at the start of the lockdown during the Covid-19 crisis, he offered advice on how to make the most of the time away from others: 'I discovered gifts and abilities I didn't know I had and they were brought out in solitude, such as an ability to write.'

Alone time also gives us the chance to pursue what interests us, what we want to become better at and learn more about. In this way, solitude can stoke our curiosity about our own betterment.

*'We need solitude, because when we're alone, we're free from obligations, we don't need to put on a show, and we can hear our own thoughts.'*
*Tamim Ansary*

Time on our own gives us space to turn possibilities over in our head, to weigh up pros and cons, to get curious about what might work and what might not, so we can make wise, well-considered decisions. Solitude, therefore, can give us greater clarity than we might otherwise have when surrounded by others.

To deepen our connection to ourselves even further, solitude also offers us the best environment in which to meditate and connect to our 'inner knowing' – that gut instinct and intuitive part of us which we may struggle to hear while in the company of others.

Albert Einstein once said, 'The intuitive mind is a sacred gift and the rational mind is a faithful servant. We have created a society that honours the servant and has forgotten the gift.' Meditation is a pathway to accessing the gift of intuition or 'inner knowing'.

### EXERCISE: Be Still and Listen to Your Inner Knowing

- Choose a quiet place where you won't be disturbed and set a timer (ideally a soft bell) to go off after 15 minutes.
- Sit upright in a comfortable position, either on a chair or on a cushion on the floor, and rest your hands in your lap. If you'd prefer to lie down, that is fine too.
- Close your eyes or direct your gaze downwards, whichever feels most comfortable.
- Inhale slowly through your nose for a count of three, hold for three, and exhale from your mouth for four. By extending the exhale you expel more breath and leave more room for a deeper inhale.

- Focus your attention on each breath as you breathe in and out.
- At any point you notice your mind wandering, pull your attention gently back to your breath, with no judgement or expectation; just keep bringing your attention back to breathing, in and out, slowly and deeply. Remember, meditation isn't about emptying your mind of thoughts; it's about practising the act of bringing your attention back to your breath whenever it wanders. This simple breathing exercise will pull you into the present moment and help you tune into your body.
- Next tune into your 'intuition' (sometimes referred to as your 'higher self') by placing your hand on your heart and breathing slowly in and out a few times. Focus your attention between your eyebrows. This is referred to as the 'third eye' or pineal gland, associated with intuition.
- Ask yourself a question – whatever you feel you're most keen to know right now. You might find it best to ask a 'yes' or 'no' question and tune in to see whether you feel a resounding 'yes' or an equally resounding 'no'. If you hear other peoples' opinions filling the space, bring your attention back to your breath and ask again.
- Notice the sensations in your body – whether you feel tension or lightness. Tune into what your body and your intuition might be telling you. You won't always get an answer, but, with practice, you'll get better at hearing and feeling your inner knowing during moments of solitude.
- Slowly open your eyes and stretch your arms up above your head. Place your hands together in a gesture of

thanks and take one more deep breath in and out before resuming your daily activities.

Instead of walking yourself through the meditation, you might prefer to use a pre-recorded audio meditation, where someone else guides you via instructions. These can be accessed via various apps (see 'Useful Resources') or YouTube, and they often come with relaxing background music too.

**EXERCISE: Uncover What Lights You Up and What Gets You Down**

Getting to know yourself better can help you make the right decisions as you journey through life and make you more comfortable in your own company. After meditating, ask yourself the following questions and write down your answers in a notebook.

- What do you most love doing and why?
- What are you most grateful for?
- If you were guaranteed to succeed, what would you try? What would you have a go at doing?
- If you were likely to fail, what would you do anyway because you love it so much?
- What do you enjoy doing so much that you often lose track of time whilst doing it?

- What places do you treasure the most?
- What activities drain your energy?

Based on your answers to the above questions, what activities do you think you could start to make more time for and do more of? Which do you think you could do less of – or delegate to someone who enjoys it more? Which places could you spend more time in?

- What behaviours and responses get you into trouble or annoy others?
- What triggers you to respond angrily or passionately? What values do you think these triggers step on? (For example if, like me, you can become defensive if you feel you've been inaccurately judged or criticized, that may be because you have a strong sense of fairness and equality.) Our reactions are so often a response to our values being compromised or challenged.

Based on your answers to the above questions, what do you think you could do to start to respond differently to certain situations?

*'Solitude is at the heart of all self-knowledge, because it is when we are alone that we learn to distinguish between the false and the true, the trivial and the important.'*
*Unknown*

## 5. Space to Navigate the Negative and Gain Fresh Perspective

*'In order to understand the world, one has to turn away from it on occasion.'*
*Albert Camus*

Time alone with your thoughts can feel threatening. In the absence of hanging out with others, you're forced to hang out with the judgmental and anxious committee inside your own head, which is not always welcome.

Yet solitude gives you the space and privacy to process your problems, to face your demons and deal with them rather than brush them under the carpet, which serves nobody.

---

Solitude gives you the space and privacy to process your problems, to face your demons and deal with them rather than brush them under the carpet, which serves nobody.

---

When you're by yourself you can privately review and release your emotions. Rather than only partially opening up to friends about something that's troubling you, or feeling uncomfortable about letting your emotions out in public, you can properly lean in and face it head on, holding nothing back, letting everything out, expressing rather than suppressing your feelings.

Crying is good for you. It lowers blood pressure and tears remove toxins and stop stress hormones like cortisol from building up.[3]

You can use your time alone to listen to what your feelings are telling you about what's getting in the way of you thriving and figure out what you might change to make yourself feel better.

You can reflect on mistakes you've made in the past, learn from them, forgive yourself or others and move on.

You can spend time alone in conversation with your inner critic, questioning and silencing that disruptive voice inside your head as you take your thoughts to court, find evidence to dispute old stories and reframe negative and often inaccurate beliefs. (See page 79 for step-by-step instructions on how to do this.)

And you can do what psychologists advise to help with anxiety – schedule in some 'worry time'. (We'll explore this a little later on.)

Fundamentally, solitude offers up this valuable opportunity to navigate through negativity, do the work and come out the other side feeling a whole lot better.

Quite fascinatingly, according to a University of Athens 2012 psychological report,[4] spending time alone has also been shown to improve empathy. Ordinarily, when we spend time with the same circle of friends or colleagues, we can develop a herd mentality or 'group think'. Whereas time alone gives us the chance to delve into individual thoughts, consider different perspectives and develop greater compassion for those outside of our friendship groups. So, if we consciously use solitude to grow, there is a beautiful irony that, in disconnecting from others, we become better at connecting with them.

If we consciously use solitude to grow, there is a beautiful irony that, in disconnecting from others, we become better at connecting with them.

*'We cannot see things in perspective until we cease to hug them to our bosom.'*
*Thomas Merton, Trappist Monk*

---

**EXERCISE: Use Worry Time to Gain Perspective**

One way to use alone time wisely is to schedule in some worry time. This involves saving worries that crop up during the day to give our attention to later, when we're by ourselves and can properly consider all the facts. During your 'worry time' you can:

1. Consider the most outlandish worst-case scenario. Then consider the equally outlandish best-case scenario. Now consider the most **likely** scenario and focus on that. Do this each time you find yourself defaulting to the worst. For example, let's say your client has told you they are

not ready to hire you to work on a big project you'd been planning. So you instantly start to worry about your income, which spirals into thinking about the worst-case scenario – you don't earn anything for a few months and end up losing your house and becoming homeless. Highly unlikely. The equally unlikely best-case scenario is that, instead of that project, your client is gearing up to invite you to work on a series of much bigger projects that are so lucrative you never need work for anyone else again. Then, reign in that perspective and consider the most likely scenario – your client will call you back in a month or two ready to start on the project or another client will hire you instead.

2. Fact-check your worries by running through what you know to be true about a situation, rather than letting your imagination run away with you. For example, in relation to the same worry about the client dropping you – remind yourself that the client has said they're not ready to hire you *yet*. They haven't said they'll never hire you. Remind yourself you have strong credentials and plenty of contacts and will likely find another project on which to work soon enough.

Using these kinds of mind tools during our alone time can make solitude constructive and valuable.

## 6. Space to Dream and Plan Goals

Solitude gives you space to plant seeds of ideas in your imagination then water them, fertilize them and watch them become seedlings of potentiality. It gives you the space to ponder possibilities, consider opportunities and plan potential eventualities. When you spend time by yourself, you can bring something from that initial light-bulb moment to reality, because, often, with less distraction, you can follow a train of thought more easily and completely.

You can close your eyes and dream; you can visualize in your mind's eye what you hope to achieve and then figure out how you intend to make it happen, plotting your route forward and creating a road map towards your destination.

In this way, time alone can be well spent. Daydreaming with intent and without interruption can get you further towards your desired destination, and I don't just mean where you want to go on holiday (although that can be a nice thing to visualize). I'm talking about the bigger goals, like the kind of home you'd like to live in, the kind of people you'd like to have in your life, the hobbies you'd like to master and the kind of career you'd like to have in five or ten years' time; the work and life ambitions you'd like to achieve.

### EXERCISE: Visualize with Intention

Visualization takes place in the cerebral cortex – the same area where our thinking, language and problem-solving happens. For this reason, the brain can't tell the difference between what it thinks about and what it sees, so it reacts to visualized images as though they are real. This is a little like how, when we imagine something we fear, our heart rate quickens as if what we fear is in front of us. The same is true when we visualize something positive.

- Imagine your desired future in your mind's eye, as if it's already happening. Focus on how you feel in your body having achieved your goal. Vividly picture yourself enjoying your accomplishment. Sketch the vision out in your mind – who's with you and what are you saying to them? See yourself living this dream life and feel the emotion that goes with that image.
- Now visualize yourself taking the steps that got you to that destination. See yourself in the process of achieving your goal.
- Imagine yourself telling someone else how proud you feel about achieving this goal and describing how you got there. See your success and feel it.

## 7. Enhanced Creativity

*'Solitude is the soil in which genius is planted, creativity grows, and legends bloom.'*
*Mike Norton*

Privacy enables creativity. This is perhaps why so many artists work in private studios or take themselves off to a woodland cabin to write. It's far easier to let your mind wander and wonder when you're by yourself.

Conversely, avoiding solitude can have a detrimental effect on one's creativity, as psychologist Mihaly Csikszentmihalyi, author of *Flow*, discovered in 1994 when he found that adolescents who can't stand being alone often stop pursuing their creative talents.[5]

Solitude has often been credited as a catalyst for creativity. Pablo Picasso famously said, 'Without great solitude, no serious work is possible.' While Albert Einstein talked about how 'the monotony and solitude of a quiet life stimulates the creative mind'.

Indeed, many creative geniuses over the centuries have said isolation directly enabled them to contribute towards making the world a better place, whether via their creations, their theories or their art.

Had the likes of Sir Isaac Newton, Einstein or Picasso been regularly interrupted and disturbed by other people's noise, they may not have had their 'eureka' moments, nor the opportunity to collect their thoughts and develop the ideas which led to their creations.

Writers, spiritual leaders, artists and philosophers tend to work best in solitude and do their best work alone. We know this because so many have reported this being so, but also because it makes sense. After all, when you're alone it is easier to concentrate, hear your thoughts and to lose oneself in creative activity.

As one of the most important inventors of all time, Nikola Tesla (who invented commercial electricity), wisely said, 'The mind is sharper and keener in seclusion and uninterrupted solitude. Originality thrives in seclusion free of outside influences beating upon us to cripple the creative mind. Be alone – that is the secret of invention: be alone, that is when ideas are born.' While Johann Wolfgang von Goethe noted, 'One can be instructed in society, one is inspired only in solitude.'

### EXERCISE: Harness Creativity as a Means of Self-Expression

Art can be used as therapy to tap into emotions that may be too tricky to express in words, and a blank piece of paper can provide the perfect opportunity for self-expression.

- Grab a blank piece of paper and some felt-tip pens, paints or colouring pencils.
- Before you draw or paint anything, shut your eyes and consider a challenge you are currently facing. Define it with some keywords.
- Now you can express yourself on the page: doodle, draw or free-write poetry or prose – just stay open to letting whatever comes up flow through your pen, pencil or paintbrush onto the page.
- Use colours which capture your feelings and write words or draw pictures that symbolize you overcoming that challenge. There's no need to critique or edit what you're doing – just give yourself the freedom of expression. Follow your imagination. Ditch your inner critic and watch what unfolds on the page.

You can choose to frame or bin this piece of art, it's entirely up to you. That's the beauty of exploring your creativity alone: *you* decide what to do with the results. Regardless of what you choose to do with it, hopefully this exercise will spark a curiosity in you to play creatively again from time to time, to pick up the paint brushes, colouring pens, camera or writing pad more often and just play.

## Your Key Takeaways

When you can't share your news, ideas or experiences with anyone and feel lonely as a result of a lack of companionship, you can choose to make the best of what you *do* have: time, space and freedom to develop ideas and learn new things. There is always a more positive perspective to consider; a different lens through which to see a situation. Solitude gives you the chance to do just that, giving you:

1. **Freedom to do as You Please.** When you're by yourself, you're in charge and in control. And, if you devote your alone time to doing activities which nourish and contribute to your thriving, you'll be better able to move the dial from lonely to content in solitude.
2. **Connection with the Present.** Solitude enables you to tune in more deeply to the world around you; seeing the world more vividly, noticing how you feel in your body and enjoying each moment more mindfully. You can use your breath and your senses to ground you to the present moment to make the most of now, especially when you're alone.
3. **Freedom to be Yourself.** The expectations and opinions of others can become noisy, so it's useful to spend time alone to turn up the volume on your own voice, uncover your own strengths, values and opinions and gain confidence in being all that you are.
4. **Connection with Yourself.** Solitude gives you the space to get to know yourself and what matters to you most, so you can make choices which satisfy and serve you well and flourish. Introspection and meditation too are best done alone; both are gifts which enable you to slow down, tune in and find answers within yourself.

5. **Space to Navigate the Negative and Gain Perspective.** Only when you're alone can you spend time working on yourself, deal with issues which have been bothering you and figure out solutions. Alone time offers the chance to work through worries, consider different perspectives and emerge the other side, feeling better.

6. **Space to Dream and Plan Goals.** It's possible to map out potential futures with other people, but only you can see inside your mind, so only you can visualize exactly what you want to achieve. Solitude gifts you the space to paint a picture in your mind's eye and create a clear vision of your desired destination.

7. **Enhanced Creativity.** Solitude is an integral habit which creative people agree is needed in order to create great works of art. And while collaboration can be useful in creative endeavours, being able to focus and concentrate on creative work and to let creative ideas flow naturally requires a quiet environment, one without distraction.

If you have only seen aloneness as something to fear or dislike, I hope you can now see solitude in a more positive light, as a useful, supportive and somewhat necessary state of being alone without being lonely. For when we surrender to the benefits of being alone, we can discover how to belong to ourselves, rather than needing to belong elsewhere.

# CHAPTER 4

# CONNECT WITH YOURSELF

*'Loneliness is a sign you're in desperate need of yourself.'*
*Rupi Kaur*

## Your Most Important Relationship

Humans are wired for connection. Yet, while longevity studies[1] reveal having people we can count on positively impacts our life satisfaction and capacity to thrive, the most important relationship we have is actually the one we have with ourselves. After all, people may come and go, but you will always have yourself; that's who you'll spend your whole life with, which is why your relationship with yourself is the most constant, enduring and vital relationship of all.

Your relationship with yourself is the most constant, enduring and vital relationship of all.

This is why the antidote to loneliness isn't just to connect with others, but to connect first with yourself – to get to know, accept and care for *you*.

If you can use your time alone to improve your relationship with yourself, and to improve how you see yourself, you can turn loneliness – something inherently painful and challenging – into something worthwhile. First, though, before embarking on your journey to foster deeper internal connection, it's worth understanding the impact of external feedback from others on your own sense of self-worth.

## The Validation Trap

Since our tribal beginnings, when acceptance or rejection from the tribe could mean life or death, external validation has mattered. This is why external opinion carries so much weight – it's an evolutionary trait. It's also how we develop and learn. As such, other people's opinions have been shaping how we see ourselves since childhood. Ever since we were born we've relied on external validation from others to help us learn how to behave and to evaluate how well we are doing. 'Look, Mummy!' we'd say, seeking recognition and approval.

As we've grown, we've continued to seek encouragement and validation from parents, teachers, bosses and peers to tell us we're on the right track; that we look, perform and achieve well enough. This has since been replaced by social media posts, follows and 'likes', as we post images to show how well we're doing in anticipation of reassurance and acceptance, to confirm we have what it takes and to prove ourselves as good and worthy of love and success.

Other times this innate need for external validation shows up in our desire for recognition and promotion at work, for praise from our friends or for compliments from our spouses.

Ultimately, if people approve, we feel good; if people don't, we feel bad. But the feel-good feeling is only fleeting compared with the longer-lasting negative feeling of perceived disapproval. Not measuring up can get us down.

Unfortunately, the more external validation we're given, the more we tend to rely on these affirmations as we grow. And therein lies the problem of this validation rollercoaster – the reliance of external feedback means your own opinion of yourself is shaped by what others might think rather than what your own inner GPS navigation (your feelings) tell you. This is when external validation becomes maladaptive, when we come to rely on this external feedback to determine our own sense of value, when we ascribe our entire self-worth to what others think and say about us.

In doing this we literally put our self-worth into other peoples' hands, passing control for how we feel about ourselves over to 'them', the subjective opinions of others – sometimes complete strangers who don't even know us at all! Meanwhile, we ignore our inner truth as we push down our feelings, even though they are signals, showing us what matters most. If only we'd pay more attention to this internal guidance over external judgements. (You'll learn how in this chapter.) Especially as those external judgements are often wholly inaccurate (which is rather ironic given that the dictionary definition of the word 'validation' is 'the action of proving the validity or accuracy of something').

What we don't tend to realize is that the way people respond to us is based on multiple influences of their own, none of which have anything to do with us – their own experiences and memories, what mood they're in that day, who we remind them of.

For example, someone might take an instant dislike to you when you're wearing your hair in a tight bun, which reminds them of the teacher who embarrassed them in front of their whole year group when they were seven. Or, if they're having a bad day, your cheeriness might annoy them when, ordinarily, they'd appreciate (and validate) it by returning your smile. Or perhaps they feel uncomfortable giving praise as it's not in their nature and makes them feel vulnerable, so they use banter and jokey criticism instead, which says more about them than you. But you'll still internalize those responses, despite them having very little to do with you at all.

What's more, most of the time what we think others *might* think about us is way off the mark and based on our own assumptions and insecurities, on what social psychologist C. H. Cooley and Han-Joachim Schubert call 'the Looking Glass Self'. As they say in their book *On Self and Social Organization*, 'I am not what I think I am and I am not what you think I am; I am what I think that you think I am.'[2]

Unfortunately, the human brain is very good at jumping to conclusions. Without external approval we often *assume* disapproval, and feeling disapproved of can lead to feelings of insecurity, unworthiness and shame. Consequently, that can make us behave in ways not true to ourselves just to please others, based on what we think they want, even though we can't know for sure what that is. Meanwhile, they are doing exactly the same. Because while we're wasting time worrying what others think of us, they're giving no thought to us at all because they're too busy worrying what we think of them! External validation is mutual; it goes both ways.

## External Voices Become Our Inner Critic

External feedback is incredibly powerful in influencing our own deep-rooted thoughts and beliefs, which become our own mental models. These are the stories we tell ourselves about the world and our place within it which, despite often being inaccurate, become true for us, trapping us in old ways of thinking.

For example, the teacher who told you that your artwork wasn't good enough may have led you to believe there was little point pursuing a creative career. So, rather than practising and improving, you gave up drawing completely. Yet the teacher may have been basing their opinion on how closely you followed the brief, rather than how good the piece was, or they might have simply been having a bad day. Yet you internalized the negative feedback and it impacted your thoughts about yourself to become 'I'm not very good at art.' Repeated over time, this thought became a belief which influenced your decisions and career choice. What a shame that the power we hand over to other people can literally affect the trajectory of our lives.

Wider society and the media, with their stereotypes, expectations and unattainable standards, can have a similar impact.

Our own internal mind chatter tends to be shaped by the way we've been spoken to over our lifetime, whether discouraging or encouraging, by our parents, teachers and peers. In general, the more we've been exposed to overt criticism and rejection, the louder our inner critical voice becomes. While the more we've been exposed to praise and encouragement, the more we may crave external validation.

## Motivation or Demoralization?

The way we've been spoken to is key, because encouragement about making improvements can motivate us to persevere, while discouragement can demoralize, restrict and limit us for fear of the shame of rejection and invalidation, so we give up. This feedback subsequently determines whether we see ourselves as capable or incapable, likeable or unlikeable.

If we're lonely, this can do us more harm than good, because our curated self-view makes our world feel like either a positive place filled with possibilities or a difficult place filled with challenges.

Knowing this, do you really want to let another person's (often assumed or inaccurate) perception of you shape how you feel about yourself?

## The Good News

Thankfully, thoughts are not set in stone, and our malleable minds can be moulded. The good news is that the neuroplasticity of our brains (i.e. the way our brain forms new synaptic connections in response to learning) means we can carve out new neural pathways (thought processes) and new beliefs by repeating more accurate and helpful thoughts more often.

That is what you shall learn to do in this chapter. This is important work, because the way you think can determine whether you become your own worst enemy or your own best ally. And when you're feeling lonely, it's important to be the latter.

So, although this need for external validation is wired into you from birth, it is possible to regain some control.

Knowing how external validation works means you're already one step ahead. The next step is to invest some alone time getting to know yourself better, so you can define what matters most to *you* rather than other people. Only then can you let go of putting your entire self-worth into the hands of others. To do this, we will look at how you can:

1. Develop self-acceptance and validate yourself
2. Practice self-compassion
3. Tune into your internal GPS navigation system (feelings)
4. Counter your negativity bias

5. Talk back to your inner critic
6. Gain self-knowledge via self-reflection
7. See alone time as 'me time'

## 1. Develop Self-Acceptance and Validate Yourself

*'The root of true confidence grows from our ability to be*
*in unconditional friendship with ourselves.'*
Pema Chodron

Self-acceptance can be one of the most radically empowering strategies to lift yourself out of loneliness. Instead of wishing *others* understood and valued you, self-acceptance helps you reclaim your power as you seek to understand, encourage and appreciate yourself. Through doing this work you learn that nobody can validate you as well as you can, which frees you from needing other people's approval as much and brings more balance to your sense of worth.

Self-acceptance can be one of the most radically empowering
strategies to lift yourself out of loneliness.

Gradually you become more willing to trust your own experiences and feelings, rather than relying on others to make you feel good about yourself, so you can go ahead and make whatever changes to your life feel right, because no longer being bound by external validation means other people's approval no longer limits and restricts you.

Also, when *you* accept all that you are, it becomes easier to allow others their reactions, which has the bonus effect of making connection with others less of a daunting prospect.

What's more, when external input matters less, any negative feedback you do receive can be used as motivation to help you improve and grow rather than seeing it only as judgement to bring you down.

Self-acceptance means accepting yourself exactly as you are right now, warts and all. To find a healthy level of self-acceptance you'll need to consider the parts that you (and others) tend to criticize and judge the most, which means accepting your imperfections as well as the parts you are happier with.

Making peace with your flaws rather than defaulting to disliking or wanting to fix them doesn't stop you from working on self-improvement. It simply means your desire for betterment is not driven by shame, guilt or criticism. When you accept and approve of yourself, any desire for self-improvement is merely personal growth born out of self-respect.

By validating yourself, you're choosing acceptance over resistance. Rather than beating yourself up for not being good enough or for making mistakes, you see yourself through a kinder lens and accept yourself as imperfectly human, learning and therefore growing with each mistake made.

### EXERCISE: Celebrate Yourself

The aim of this exercise is to uncover how far you've come, even if it may not always feel that way, and to give yourself the recognition and praise you deserve. Part of self-acceptance is self-approval, which involves noticing and appreciating your light.

- **List all the times you've successfully dealt with life's challenges.** For example, you may have persisted to get a job in a certain industry despite many rejections; or perhaps you've overcome a fear of heights to climb a mountain; or maybe you have managed to sustain a safe and loving environment for your children despite going through a difficult divorce. Next to those examples, list the character strengths or skills you used to help you cope: from hope and grit to kindness and leadership.

- **Celebrate tiny wins.** Now write down some smaller victories worth celebrating that have happened over the past week (it could be anything from managing not to burn the dinner or completing a yoga class, finishing a book you've been meaning to read or completing your tax return). Write down how you'll celebrate these small daily or weekly wins, perhaps by rewarding yourself with a takeaway meal, a bowl of ice cream or listening to your favourite album uninterrupted. You deserve it!

- **Celebrate your superpowers.** List some of the things you are good at (for example, listening, building, organizing or sorting). Choose one of these skills as your 'superpower'. Now list a few things you've achieved or done well (i.e. being a prefect at school and coming third in a talent show, as well as more recent achievements). Jot down the choices you're proud of (i.e. choosing to apply for that job or going to that university, or choosing to live where you do). Revisit Chapter 3 and list your character strengths, along with any other positive words that define your personality and the way you show up in the world. Read this list whenever you're feeling unworthy or down to remind yourself of your greatness.

**EXERCISE: Characterize Yourself**

This exercise serves as a reminder that our imperfections are what make us human. Consider this: when you read a book or watch a movie, which characters do you like the most? Those with relatable flaws who trip up on their way to work or who can't find their car keys under the mess on their desk, or the seemingly flawless characters who never put a foot wrong and never have a hair out of place? Most likely you'll prefer the former, because imperfections make characters more personable, relatable and likeable. Given how much we all want to be liked, how ironic it is that we try to hide our imperfections and worry about being judged for our flaws when they are precisely what make us human and more likeable than perfection ever could! So, let's embrace them.

- **List your flaws and imperfections.** What would you change about yourself if you could? For example, perhaps you're impatient or untidy (like me), or perhaps you'd prefer to be taller, fitter or have better posture (also like me)?

- **List ways you could improve your weaknesses or smooth out your imperfections if you chose to.** Some perceived flaws may be impossible to change (your height for example). But how might you be pro-active to change the things you have a hard time accepting about yourself? If there are ways you can become better at something and grow, try them. Otherwise, accept them as part of your unique and wonderful self and celebrate them rather than trying to change them.

- **List past mistakes you've been dwelling on.** Next to the mistake write down what you've learned from it and use that as a positive. We all make mistakes; they're how we learn and grow. We learn far more from when things go wrong than when we succeed, and it's important to consider what you might do differently next time; beating yourself up for making mistakes serves no one. Permit them, accept them, learn from them, then move on. Give yourself permission to be human rather than superhuman.

- **Forgive yourself.** Sit with your struggles as a compassionate observer. Think about what has been said and done, then write an apology as you consider what you could still do to make amends or learn from your mistake. You can keep your forgiveness note as a reminder or throw it away and let it go. Remember that we all do things we are not proud of; as long as we learn from them, it's okay.

*'You have been criticizing yourself for years, and it hasn't worked. Try approving of yourself and see what happens.'*
*Louise Hay*

## 2. Practice Self-Compassion

> *'You cannot be lonely if you like the person you're alone with.'*
> *Wayne Dyer*

I have good news. Learning to like who you already are is much less work than trying to be someone else.

What's more, the more you appreciate and value yourself, the less tolerance you have for people who don't. So, when you *do* connect with others and lift yourself out of loneliness, you'll be drawn to those who treat you well. Conversely, if you don't treat yourself well, it can be difficult to attract others into your life who'll treat you with the respect and love you deserve.

Self-compassion is different to self-esteem, because having good self-esteem means we feel good about ourselves, especially when we're doing well, but less so when we're doing less well. In contrast, self-compassion doesn't evaluate or judge; it simply allows us to *be*.

As renowned self-compassion expert Kristin Neff says, 'When we fail, self-esteem deserts us, which is precisely when we need it most.' Self-compassion is there for us during those tougher times. When we get things wrong, it gives us permission to be human, because getting things wrong is what all humans do.

We need to befriend ourselves; to take care of us in the same way we'd take care of a dear friend who was struggling.

To cultivate more compassion for ourselves we need to befriend ourselves; to take care of us in the same way we'd take care of a dear friend who was struggling.

**EXERCISE: Look at Yourself in the Mirror**

We look in the mirror every day to brush our teeth, but how often do we really look at ourselves properly? How often do we look ourselves in the eyes and really see *us*?

- Be gentle with yourself. Each morning for the next few days say: 'I've got you. I understand you. You're okay.' It may feel strange at first. If you feel uncomfortable, consider why that might be.
- After a few days, say, 'I love you,' adding, 'I respect you and I'll always try to do what's right for you.' If that's too weird, you can try other variations – for example: 'I care about you' or 'I'll do my best to take better care of you from now on.' This exercise helps you connect deeply with yourself.

**EXERCISE: Practice a 'Loving Kindness' Meditation**

- To get into a meditative state, sit comfortably and inhale slowly, then exhale, focusing on your breath.
- Repeat this a few times then bring to mind someone you care deeply for. It could be anyone from your past or your present, even a beloved pet. Feel that sense of warmth and care that you have for them and focus on it.
- Picture a ball of light around your heart as you feel loving kindness for this beloved other. Say in your head, 'May you be well, may you be safe from harm, may you live

your life with ease, may you be happy,' and visualize the golden light flow from your heart to theirs.

- Repeat this mantra as you call to mind someone you have a less positive relationship with, someone who misunderstands you or may be angry or upset and need a dose of kindness sent their way. Picture the golden light flow from your heart to theirs.

- Repeat the mantra again, this time sending loving kindness out to a wider group of people, the people who live in your neighbourhood, and the wider world. See the golden light emanate out to touch all of them.

- Finally, bring this mantra back to yourself. Put your hand on your heart and say, 'May you be well, may you be safe from harm, may you live your life with ease, may you be happy.' Sit with that feeling of loving kindness for yourself for a while as you slowly inhale and exhale.

### EXERCISE: Create a Ritual to Check in with Yourself Regularly

For the next month, at a time that suits you (set a reminder if you need to), take a deep breath in and out and then:

- **Ask yourself how you're feeling.** If it helps, speak to yourself like you would a small child or best friend. If they were feeling troubled or anxious about something, you'd suggest you talk it through. What has been bothering you or pleasing you so far today? Write down your thoughts. Pay attention to your response and to how your body feels. Do you have a flutter of anxiety or excitement in your chest? Do you feel heavy or light?

- **Ask yourself what you need.** If a child or friend was feeling too highly strung to be able to do so, if they needed to calm down first, you'd suggest they have a drink of water and get some fresh air or go out for a little walk. If they were feeling sad about something, you'd encourage them to let it all out and have a good cry. If they were feeling tired, you'd suggest a comforting cup of hot chocolate and an early night. Go ahead and give yourself what you need to nourish rather than numb you. Repeat this every day for a month to deepen your self-compassion and flex your self-care muscles.

Befriending ourselves means turning that thoughtfulness inward and looking out for ourselves rather than being down on ourselves. This takes practice, but only when we befriend ourselves can we begin to feel more worthy of connection with others.

*'If you make friends with yourself, you'll never be alone.'*
*Maxwell Maltz*

## 3. Tune Into Your Internal GPS Navigation System (Feel Your Feelings)

Our feelings are essentially signals which exist to guide us, yet we often choose to push them down and ignore them, heeding other people's opinions rather than our own inner knowledge. Given how much impact external validation has on our life choices and sense of worth, shouldn't we pay more attention to our own internal sources of feedback – our own vital signposts?

Positive emotions signal for us to do more of whatever is making us feel good; negative emotions are showing us something else. They are there to teach us; to either flag up the need to change and do something differently or to highlight a need to process those feelings, so we can move on.

Yet many people are conditioned not to feel their feelings – to push them away and ignore them, to suppress them rather than express them – and this repression can and often does lead to depression.

Constantly distracting ourselves from our own minds and feelings can be unhealthy. When we push our feelings down, it's a bit like pushing a beach ball under water; they will just pop up time and time again until they are dealt with. To heal, we need to feel, because while our thoughts are not facts, our feelings are genuinely felt and deserve an audience.

Unfortunately, with so much pressure on us to be constantly happy, it's not uncommon to see negative emotions as bad. But negative feelings like sadness, anger, jealousy and guilt are all part of the human spectrum of emotion. They are part of what it means to be human. A life devoid of them would not be real. Without the rain there would be no rainbow; without leaning into our sorrow, we cannot appreciate true happiness. In order to flourish and thrive, we need to give ourselves permission to feel *all* the feelings on the spectrum of emotion rather than dismiss negative ones, however brutal, to express them rather than repress them. Releasing our negative emotions releases their hold over us, as does labeling them.

A 2007 University of California fMRI (Functional Magnetic Resonance Imaging) study called 'Putting Feelings into Words' assessed the activation of the emotional side of the brain (the amygdala) by detecting changes associated with blood flow. The study found that the emotional reaction of participants who had been shown images of emotional expressions reduced when they were invited to name the emotion they saw.[3] Labelling emotions in this way can lessen their weight and is a technique that has even been employed by FBI hostage-negotiators to calm situations down.

## EXERCISE: Feel Feelings and Tune Into Their Signal

It's not always easy to really feel our feelings, especially if we've spent so long avoiding them. But there are ways to tap into them and use them as the valuable sources of internal feedback that they are.

- **Label how you are feeling** in the moment by naming the emotions in your head or out loud, or write them down. For example, 'I feel disappointed,' or 'That's made me really angry.'
- **Now consider what your feelings might be signalling for you to do.** Which choice do they want you to make? Which values might they be responding to? For

example, if you feel angry when someone is dishonest, that flags up how much you value honesty. When you feel disappointed by a lack of commitment, it may signal how important friendship and respect are to you. Your feelings signal what matters most to you. Consider actions you could take as a result. For example, if you are feeling constantly disappointed when social plans are cancelled at the last minute, might there be a way you can reach out to help the person cancelling to commit? Maybe you could suggest doing something together which fits in with something they are already doing (such as joining them when they take their child to football practice, so you can have a coffee together from the sidelines)?

- **Ride the waves and emerge the other side.** Lean into the feelings and accept the discomfort. Cry if you feel like crying, as tears help remove the stress hormone cortisol. Punch a pillow or scream out loud if you feel angry. Get those feelings out without physically hurting you or anyone else and you'll feel better.

- **Remind yourself that setbacks strengthen us as we grow stronger as a result of coping with challenges**. Refer back to the list of challenges you've overcome that you jotted down in the 'Celebrate Yourself' exercise on page 62 and reflect on how they've shown you what you are capable of (which is likely more than you thought).

## 4. Counter Your Negativity Bias

In general, the two types of negative thought we tend to have are judgements and worries. And, as humans, we have a bias towards these types of thinking.

This negativity bias is an inbuilt evolutionary trait left over from our cave-dwelling days, when noticing our flaws helped us correct them, where putting one foot wrong could mean danger or death for everyone in our tribe.

Similarly, worrying about worst-case scenarios was useful when danger genuinely lurked around each corner. It was far better for our survival to wrongly assume a sabre-tooth tiger was hiding and about to pounce than optimistically assume it wasn't and risk being eaten.

Consequently, our evolutionary past means we often focus on, and react more strongly to, negative situations, comments or events than positive ones. Our brains haven't been trained to respond to positive stimuli as strongly. So, we'll focus on what might go wrong in the future and what we've done wrong in the past, rather than what might go right and what we've done well.

As a survival mechanism, pain and danger were prioritized in our memory bank above joy and pleasure, which were superfluous to our survival. So, judgement and anxiety used to serve us: we needed our negativity bias to focus on the negative and alert our brains to danger so our bodies could optimally function and face that danger. And as soon as our brains are alerted to potential danger, our bodies prepare: our lungs make space for more oxygen; our heartbeat quickens to pump oxygenated blood to the brain where it's needed most, to sharpen our senses and muscles in anticipation to fight or take flight; and our energy is rationed.

These days, the danger of death has diminished, yet our evolutionary bias and critical inner voice has remained. As neuroscientist Rick Hanson says, our brains continue to 'respond more intensely to unpleasant things than to equally pleasant ones'.[4]

So, what can we do to counter this?

In the 1970s, Robert Levenson and Dr Gottman began conducting longitudinal studies of couples who they invited to solve a relational conflict within 15 minutes. They reviewed the conversations between the couples and were able to predict those couples who stayed together and those who did not with over 90% accuracy when they followed up with the participating couples nine years later.[5]

As a result of this study, the pair came up with what is now widely known in psychology as 'the magic ratio' for sustainable relationships, which is that it can take as many as five positive interactions to repair one negative one. This tells us that, in order to counter negativity – whether it comes from external or internal sources – we need to deliberately take in positive stimuli, encouraging comments and joyful experiences by noticing, seeking and savouring the good (five times as much). This helps us counter our negativity bias as we work to remember and store positive emotions.

The additional bonus of generating positive emotions is what positivity researcher Barbara Fredrickson calls the 'broaden and build' effect. Over two decades of research, she discovered that over time, the more positive emotions we have, the more we can build up a well of positivity to dip into during times of adversity and the more resilient we become. Via MRI scans, Frederickson also found that positive emotions enable us to think with clarity and accuracy, as we remain open to solutions. Conversely, negative emotions shut down our logical neocortex (the part of the brain responsible for logical thinking, spatial reasoning and sensory perception), which restricts our thinking power and traps us in negative spirals of inaccurate perceptions and misinterpretation. So, by finding ways to generate positive emotions, we are better able to think more clearly and solve the problems we are worrying about.[6]

---

**EXERCISE: Focus on the Good**

Often, when we give ourselves a hard time or focus on something negative, our minds get carried away in a negative spiral and, before we know it, everything seems far worse than it really is. Our negativity bias also means we have a natural tendency to ruminate on past regrets or worry about the future rather than enjoy the present. To counter this:

- **Create a gratitude journal**. Gratitude is a useful counter to negativity. For seven days, at the start or end of each day, purposely seek and savour the good. List everything you are grateful for now. Sometimes, on difficult lonely days it can be hard to find much to appreciate, but it's there if you look for it. There's always something to be grateful for; whether it is your health, nature, a pet, a life filled with good memories, hope, being able to walk and see and hear, a roof over your head, breathing, food, tea and coffee, a specific person or place, having the chance to start again tomorrow. Write down anything you appreciate having in your life or anything good that happened today. For example, your boss may have pulled you up on something and made you feel bad, but when you got home your dog was so pleased to see you that you had the best cuddle, so you feel grateful for having a pet. Or perhaps an event you were looking forward to attending was rained off, but that gave you the opportunity to complete a book you've not had time to finish reading. Maybe after watching the news you just feel glad to live in a peaceful, low-crime area. By focusing on what you *do* have, rather than on what you don't have yet, you boost your positive emotion. After the initial seven days is up, continue recording what you're grateful for as a pleasant regular ritual at whichever time of day or week suits you best.

- **Practice using gratitude in real time.** Each time you notice yourself embarking on a negative spiral of thoughts about what's wrong, remind yourself about what's right. Take a deep breath in and list three things you have to be grateful for. Another way to do this exercise is to photograph anything that gives you a positive feeling, which you can look back on whenever you need a lift.

- **Record your wins.** For the next seven days, write down something you have achieved each day. This will help your mind learn to focus on what you *have* managed to do rather than on what you have failed to do. So, rather than berate yourself for failing to go to the gym, celebrate the fact you went for a long walk. And rather than criticize yourself for eating a bag of crisps, congratulate yourself for having had five pieces of fruit or vegetables. At the end of the week, reward yourself for all you've accomplished – and consider how much better you feel than when you stress over everything you've *not* managed to do.

## 5. Talk Back to Your Inner Critic

It's a common mistaken belief that the better you get to know yourself, the worse you'll feel about yourself, because you'll uncover all your nasty faults and negative thoughts. Yet the converse tends to be true.

When you take time to tune in to your thoughts and feel your feelings, you get the opportunity to challenge negative notions and reframe inaccurate beliefs with a more positive and accurate self-view. It may be easier to ignore thoughts and feelings for fear of what you might find. But doing the work to shift your attitude is worthwhile, as your new way of thinking can become habitual and helpful.

## How Thoughts Work

When you understand how your thoughts work and what you can do about your inbuilt negativity bias, you can talk back to your inner critic and master your mind to work with you rather than against you.

Thoughts are not facts. Thoughts are essentially neurons firing together. The more often you repeat certain thoughts, neural pathways are created which cause them to become beliefs; the stories you tell yourself. So beliefs are thoughts you've repeated often.

These repetitive thoughts have, in the main, come directly or been influenced via external sources – society, media, peers and family. And these repeated perceptions (which are not facts) sink into your psyche and become your core beliefs, or your mental model.

As such, they strongly inform your opinion of yourself and how you show up in the world. When you don't explore them, you default to them. And, given how many tend to be negative and inaccurate, this is not particularly helpful to your wellbeing.

Your critical inner voice doesn't wish you any harm, though. Quite the contrary: your judgemental mind chatter has good intentions and is simply trying to protect you from the shame and embarrassment of other people's scorn and rejection.

The problem is, because of the severe impact mistakes and rejection used to have from an evolutionary perspective (see page 73), your inner critic has been wired to get warning messages to you quickly. So it uses a stick rather than a carrot approach. Rather than gently motivating you to do better, it harshly warns you, saying: 'You can't do that. What will people think?' So you don't bother trying, which further feeds your belief that you're not good enough. Or, when you do something which might lead to a negative judgement, your inner critic berates you, saying, 'Why did you have to say/do that? You're such an idiot,' and so on. Consequently, you end up being incredibly unfair on yourself.

Ironically, this means your judgemental inner critic can cause the very thing it is trying to protect you from, as the critical commentary can make you feel unworthy of connection, thus disconnecting and withdrawing from others, amplifying your loneliness.

Yet we rarely question the validity of our mind-chatter. Instead, we accept our thoughts as truths and end up basing our actions and behaviour on those judgements. Our lives become dictated by inaccurate beliefs generated by a part of our brain which is stuck in the Stone Age.

So what can you do about this outdated system which, despite trying to protect you, is being more of a hindrance than a help? How can you regulate what you've been hardwired to automate?

Now you know your critical inner voice is skewed, you can dispute your judgemental thoughts. And solitude offers you a valuable opportunity to do this. Rather than accept these damning negative voices, which can detrimentally affect your behaviour, having the space to notice and listen to them also gives you time to question and reframe them.

By doing so, you can move from judgement to compassion, take inaccurate thoughts 'to court', collect evidence for and against them, and reframe the beliefs which no longer serve you.

Here's how...

---

### EXERCISE: Listen, Question and Reframe

To gain control over your often automatic thought patterns and responses, you need to pay attention to them.

So, first, **listen**.

- **Try to catch yourself each time you notice a negative thought** or belief pop into your mind. Say 'stop' each time you notice your thoughts getting caught up in a negative 'spiral' to halt catastrophic thinking in its tracks. This is far easier to do when you're on your own than when you're with other people, and it works well with judgmental thoughts too.

- **Listen to how you talk to yourself and what you are saying**. Our judgmental beliefs often begin with, 'I always...' or 'I never...', 'I'm so...', 'I'm such a...' or 'They think I'm...' Pay attention to the words you use and the tone of your inner voice. Make a list of these judgmental beliefs and negative thoughts in a notebook or record details on your phone's voice recorder.

- **Consider where those thoughts and beliefs may have stemmed from**. For example, 'I'm always late. What's wrong with me?' may be an observation other people have made about you or maybe something you feel bad about yourself. 'I'm so clumsy' may have come from your parents or spouse who has told you so, or you might have labelled yourself as such every time you drop something.

Next, **question** and **validate**.

- **Take your thoughts to court.** Question them, dispute them; seek evidence for and against them. For example, are you really 'always' late? Perhaps you are often late because you optimistically think you have more time than you actually have. Perhaps when you do leave yourself more time to get ready, you're early or on time. Try to remember those instances when you've not been late. There's bound to be some evidence against the claim that you're *always* late for every single event. (You've already completed a similar exercise to deal with anxious thoughts when you considered the worst-case scenario and best-case scenario, then returned to the most likely – and far less worrying – scenario in the 'Using Worry Time to Gain Perspective' exercise on page 46.)
- **Validate your thoughts.** Figure out which thoughts and beliefs are true and which are not by considering first what's *not* true about them. For example, as a result of not knowing your sister was upset about something, you might say, 'I'm a terrible sister.' But then, when you question that thought, you remember sending a card and flowers when she was struggling another time and realize you're there for her when she needs you and vice versa.

And perhaps this time she didn't want you to know she was upset so didn't tell you. Or maybe you believe you can only be happy if you're in a relationship because that's what you've been told. But, when you question that belief, you gather evidence to dispute it – your cousin is single and is one of the happiest people you've met, living her life on her own terms, travelling and volunteering. And perhaps you were miserable in a previous relationship – more evidence to counter that belief. If there is even a shred of evidence to support the inaccuracy of a thought or belief, that's one to focus on reframing.

Now, **reframe**.

- This is where you get to override the noise that is coming from an external radio station. You can replace the 'fake news' (for want of a better analogy) and replace it with more factual data. You can consider what another way of looking at something might be. Reframe thoughts you've found evidence to dispute. For example, rather than think and believe, 'I'll only be truly happy if I can find love,' you can reframe the inaccurate thought by saying to yourself, 'Lots of people are happy on their own,' or 'I felt really content when I was gardening and had nobody telling me what to do,' or 'Relationships have sometimes made me miserable, so I don't need to be in one to be happy. I can find happiness elsewhere.'
- If you struggle to reframe your inaccurate thoughts, try considering what you might say to someone else in response to them telling you their inaccurate 'truth'. For

example, what would you say to someone who told you they'll only be truly happy if they find love? You might find it easier to come up with more accurate thoughts and alternative answers may spring to mind if the belief is not centred on yourself. And they may feel more believable too. Imagine a friend telling you, 'I'm a terrible sister' and think of what you'd say in response. You'd remind her of all the times they'd been there for their sibling to counter their negative inaccurate thought with factual data to the contrary.

- Go one step further and create actions to support the validity of your new thought, to prove its accuracy. For example, perhaps you could organize a monthly get-together with your sister. Or maybe you could talk to your sister about your thought process and you could each create a wish list of places to visit, films to watch, or books to read together.

Reframing is simply replacing inaccurate and unhelpful thoughts with more accurate and helpful ones, by repeating those thoughts more often than those you've repeatedly been telling yourself. In doing so you'll create new neural pathways, new thoughts and beliefs that better serve you.

You can also reframe those thoughts which think they're protecting you but are actually preventing you from connection. The kind that stop you from contacting people – the ones that say, 'I don't want to impose' or 'I'll just be a burden' or 'I've left it too long; it'll be so awkward'.

You won't, you're not, it won't. Reframe those thoughts to consider the possibility that, 'They'll be pleased I got in touch' or 'I've got nothing to lose'. Pick up the phone, send that message, (re)connect.

## 6. Gain Self-Knowledge via Self-Reflection

Once you've unpicked which thoughts and beliefs are accurate and which aren't, it becomes easier to be your authentic self, rather than living a life where your energy is drained as you try to be who you think you *ought* to be, rather than who you truly are.

You've already completed exercises that will more readily align your actions to your values and have uncovered your strengths so you will more readily use them. Now it's time to dig deeper to consider what lights you up and matters most to *you* as an individual? (Refer back to those strengths, values and activities you uncovered during the exercises in Chapter 3.)

When you know your true nature and have a firm grasp on what matters most to you personally, you can nurture that truth and stay true to it. As such, self-awareness is a gift which helps you understand what you need in order to thrive.

*'When you lose touch with your inner stillness, you lose touch with yourself. When you lose touch with yourself, you lose yourself in the world.'*
*Eckhart Tolle*

The benefits of journaling include greater self-awareness, emotional intelligence and goal-achievement.

### EXERCISE: Journaling

Journaling is an excellent way to contemplate and get to know yourself better. The benefits of journaling include greater self-awareness, emotional intelligence and goal-achievement. The writing process helps you to make sense of jumbled thoughts, put things into perspective, come up with ideas and find solutions to problems.

Journaling can be done anytime, but it can be worth scheduling into your day even if you're busy – *especially* if you're busy. You can either find a serene space to sit peacefully and comfortably with a cup of tea and a notepad or take yourself for a walk and talk into a voice recorder, noting down your thoughts on paper on your return.

**Journal Prompts**

- Think back to when you were ten years old. What did you love to spend your time doing? Write a list of activities you enjoyed or write a diary entry from memory. Could you do any of those activities again now? For example, I loved reading alone under a tree, and it's something which retains its magical joyful feeling today. I'm also planning on taking up roller-skating again. Perhaps you loved baking, singing or dancing? Close your eyes and visualize yourself in the place you remember doing what you loved. Perhaps you thrived on stage or curled up on the sofa with a book. You may have grown and changed, but you're still you. Write down actions you can take to do more of what you loved doing as a child.

- Refer back to your gratitude journal. Read through all the things, people and places you have written down in appreciation and think for a moment about why you are grateful for them. How did they make you feel other than grateful? And can you attribute any of them to your own choices? For example, you might have felt grateful for your pet, which you can thank yourself for, as you made the decision to get one, sensibly took your time to find the right breed and you take good care of them. Thank yourself for your persistence and responsibility which led you to spend sufficient time finding the right pet for your needs. Your strengths of kindness and love are why you take your pet for regular walks, whatever the weather. This exercise will help remind you of some of the great qualities you possess which make you, you.

- Next look for any patterns in what you've written which might tell you something else about yourself. For example, you may have frequently expressed gratitude for things in the natural world, which tell you that time in nature matters to you. Or you may have noted how much you appreciate working on certain types of creative project, which suggests you might like to devote more time to those. Perhaps good books crop up often, in which case you could spend some time finding similar ones; maybe finding equally engaging books could become a personal mission and topic of conversation when you meet people or join online book discussion groups to ask if others know of any similar reads. This exercise helps you to simultaneously build self-awareness and get clear about what you appreciate most in life.

- At the end of each day this week write about something you've learned about yourself or noticed about your environment that you wouldn't have noticed had you been surrounded by others. This exercise will help you to cultivate curiosity, flex your noticing muscles and feel positive about time in solitude.
- Reflect back on your written or recorded journal notes whenever you are feeling low or lonely, or whenever you feel that you need to reconnect with your true self.

## 7. See Alone Time as 'Me Time'

*'Your relationship with yourself sets the tone for every other relationship you have.'*
*Robert Holden*

This final step is about getting more accustomed with being alone, which is important because it sometimes feels as if modern life has been designed to distract us from ourselves. In our always-on, 24/7 world, there's so much to look at, to watch and scroll through. Pre-internet, we had to physically go somewhere to connect with people outside of our homes; nowadays we're surrounded with opportunities to connect virtually and get used to this feeling of constant connection. As a result, we've almost forgotten how to be alone with ourselves.

The more time you spend on your own without feeling lonely, the more you'll rewire your neural pathways to believe alone time is positive rather than negative.

However, if we devote our alone time to doing things which lift us up, help us connect with ourselves or with the world around us, we can become accustomed to being alone without feeling lonely. And the more time you spend on your own without feeling lonely, the more you'll rewire your neural pathways to believe alone time is positive rather than negative, creating a mindset shift. That's neuroplasticity in action.

*'Like a journey to a remote region, getting accustomed to being alone is a hard road, but it's a rewarding road.'*
Terry Waite

---

**EXERCISE: Making the Most of 'Me Time'**

- **Ground yourself and connect with the world.** Place your hand on your heart and notice it beating as you breathe in and out. Tune into your own heartbeat, then think about all the other heartbeats beating across the world. We share this experience with every living thing.

Feel connected to others in this way. Then feel your feet rooted to the floor; imagine roots pulling you down. Feel grounded to the earth and connected to all those with beating hearts who walk on it too.

- **Write a thank-you card.** This is an incredible feel-good activity because it incorporates positive psychology interventions of practising gratitude with practicing kindness and creative play. Gratitude biologically affects the brain and has been called 'nature's antidepressant', given the way it boosts dopamine and oxytocin even more successfully than drugs. As such, giving thanks is a gift to both ourselves *and* the recipient. Gratitude makes us feel happy for what we have right now – the presents in our present – while sharing your gratitude with its recipient also makes them feel appreciated. Once you've written your thank-you card, either hand-deliver it or pop it in the post.

- **Watch the sunrise or sunset.** These awe-inspiring events happen every single day and yet, most of the time, we are too busy or not present enough to notice them. Choose to watch them from time to time and savour the moment.

- **Daydream**. When you're by yourself you can make the most of the silence and let your mind wander and wonder. Use your imagination to conjure up images of dreams you'd like to bring to fruition. Your daydreams will tell you a lot about what matters to you. As Terry Waite says in his book *Solitude,* 'During those years of isolation I began to travel in my head. Using my imagination I crossed continents, sailed the oceans, and retreated into the inner recesses of my mind in order to try and understand myself more completely.'[7]

- **Make plans and reminisce on fond memories.** Moments aren't just enjoyed in the moment. We can amplify them by looking forward to them, savouring them as they happen and also reminiscing on them. So make plans to give yourself something to look forward to. Rather than living life aimlessly, come up with a destination, some goals – even small ones. Write down what you'd like to do and then plan ways to make it happen. Book that gig or adventure and put the date in the diary. Then look back on past events by digging out photo albums and savouring the feel-good feelings you have around them.

- **Take yourself on a date or adventure.** Go to the cinema, zoo or theatre on your own; go kayaking or on a mini-break. Enjoy the freedom and savour the experience of not having to converse; just immerse yourself and soak up the experience.

- **Be a tourist in your home town.** Visit somewhere new in your local neighbourhood that you have never visited before. Find places of interest that you've never been to.

*'If you are never alone, you cannot know yourself.'*
*Paulo Coelho*

## Your Key Takeaways

How you see yourself and how much you value yourself greatly impacts your life, including how you feel when you're alone. This is why connecting with yourself is so important when navigating your way out of loneliness.

If you don't like or value yourself, how can you expect others to like and value you? And how can you find your people if you haven't really found yourself? Plus, if so much of your self-worth is determined by the stories you are told (by others) and the stories you tell yourself as a result, it's of critical importance to make sure those stories are true.

1. **Develop Self-Acceptance and Validate Yourself.** Given how much we rely on external feedback and validation from others to help us self-evaluate and shape our self-view, and given the assumptions and inaccuracies around this feedback, it's important to be able to self-validate; to recognize, acknowledge and accept our own experiences, feelings and ideas as being valid and valuable too. Learning to accept all that we are, including our imperfections, is crucial, because when we approve of ourselves, the approval of others becomes less restrictive.

2. **Practice Self-Compassion.** As humans we don't need to have everything figured out; we simply need to become aware of, understand and hear our needs, so that we can become our own best friend, giving ourselves the support we deserve. As a result, we don't need to rely on other people to feel good about ourselves, because we treat ourselves with care, pay attention to our own needs and grow more comfortable with giving ourselves a break.

3. **Tune in to Your Internal GPS Navigation System (Feelings).** With all the external expectations, pressures and feedback to live up to, it's lucky we have our own internal guidance system

(our feelings) to help us navigate our way through life. Taking time to tune in to how we feel is vital in helping us understand what's working for us, what isn't and where to go next.

4. **Counter Your Negativity Bias.** By focusing on what we have to be grateful for rather than on what we lack, we can pay feel-good emotions into our positivity bank, which we can draw upon to help us cope during more difficult times, including when we're feeling lonely. Positive emotions also help our cognitive functioning, so we can stay open-minded and apply logic to problems, including how to reduce loneliness.

5. **Talk Back to Your Inner Critic.** It's a comfort to know that even our harshest internal judgements have our best interests at heart and that, thanks to the neuroplasticity of our brain, we can replace inaccurate, discouraging and harmful thoughts with accurate, encouraging and helpful ones. Time alone gives us the perfect opportunity to do this important work.

6. **Gain Self-Knowledge Via Self-Reflection.** Journaling and answering questions about how we think, feel and behave are great ways to increase self-awareness. The more self-aware we become, the more consciously and intentionally we can do more of what lights us up, so we may create the feelings we want to feel and the life we hope to lead.

7. **See Alone Time as 'Me Time'.** What if it became habitual for us to see alone time as 'me time'? As an opportunity to hit the pause button, to slow down and tune back into what matters most to us, to do more of what we enjoy? What if we saw solitude as a beautiful opportunity for serenity amid the busy-ness of everyday life?

When we spend time alone, we get to give ourselves the attention we deserve. We get to respond to ourselves the way we wish others would – with love and compassion, with encouragement and respect. And the better we know ourselves, the easier it becomes to allow and accept other people's reactions, because we've reclaimed our power.

The added bonus is that *inner* connection creates a foundation for better *outer* connection too. Because the better we feel in our own company, the better we become at being in others' company.

## CHAPTER 5

# CONNECT BETTER WITH OTHERS

While loneliness can be partially remedied by better connecting with yourself and learning to find solace in solitude so you enjoy your own company, it is ultimately remedied through supportive connection with others – even just one other person – to give you the comfort and security of knowing that someone else cares.

Of course, if you are shy, have low self-esteem or social anxiety, or if you've been hurt by people in the past, you may feel uncomfortable interacting with others. So, before you go out into the world to make new connections or work on improving existing ones, it's worth investing time learning how to connect better with other people. Doing so will give you confidence and empower you to make each connection count.

Even if you are a confident communicator, there's always room for improvement when it comes to making those around you feel good and being the best friend, colleague and family member that you can be.

*'The only way to have a friend is to be one.'*
*Ralph Waldo Emerson*

## Reciprocal Good Feeling

The best relationships offer mutual care and appreciation. When people make you feel good, you want to spend more time with them, and when that feeling is reciprocated, it offers the opportunity to deepen those connections, make them truly meaningful and ultimately protect against loneliness.

Treating others as you wish to be treated yourself is a useful *modus operandi* when it comes to connecting better with those you cherish and generating the deepest and most fruitful, mutually beneficial relationships. So, if you want to be seen, heard and valued by others, you need to better see, hear and value others yourself.

If you want to be seen, heard and valued by others, you need to better see, hear and value others yourself.

As such, optimum connection is not just about better-quality connections; it's about connecting better with those you connect with. So, while finding people who make you feel good is important, so is doing what you can yourself to make other people feel good. You can do that by ensuring support is mutual and reciprocated, by making time for each other, by showing your appreciation and by listening well.

In order to optimize supportive relationships and connect better with those you interact with, it's therefore important to:

1. Listen well
2. Respond well
3. Show you care

4. Show your appreciation
5. Show willing
6. Learn the art of conversation
7. Learn to be vulnerable and cultivate trust

## 1. Listen Well

> *'The hidden world reveals itself when we listen.'*
> *Bobette Buster*

When you show an interest in people by paying attention to what they have to say, you can create a positive connection, you can get to understand them better as people and you can make them feel seen, heard and valued. So, when it comes to forming strong bonds with others, how well you listen is critical.

---

**EXERCISE: Practise Listening Well**

Communication is a two-way street, so interactions should go in both directions. For that reason, it's important to listen as much as you talk. Those who mutually and sincerely listen to each other have a deeper sense of connection than those who do not. This explains why, although valuable to have someone listen to your innermost feelings, therapy cannot replace truly reciprocated mutually supportive friendships.

- **Pay attention to what people are saying.** Next time someone is talking to you, give them your full attention, and show an interest by nodding and using your facial expressions to show you're listening (smiling when they say something good and interesting; showing concern when they share a difficult experience).

- **Maintain eye contact and stay present.** Don't spend the time planning what you want to say in response. Look directly at them instead of looking away at something that's caught your eye or, even worse, at your phone. When someone is talking to you, they deserve your full and undivided attention, just as you do when you speak to them.

## 2. Respond Well

How you respond to what people say to you can strongly impact how you make them feel. Indeed, while you may know how to respond to people's bad news – with gentle sympathy and care, nodding and showing empathy – most of us haven't been taught how to respond to other people's good news, which, according to research conducted at the University of California and published by the American Psychological Association,[1] is an even more critical determinant of a strong relationship.

How you respond to what people say to you can strongly impact how you make them feel.

The only positive way to respond to good news is with mutual interest, celebration and encouragement. This method of response is called 'active constructive' response and makes the speaker feel like you're genuinely interested, that you want to know more, and it heightens their joy rather than dilutes it. As well as bolstering their own good feelings when you respond in this way, you'll also reap the benefits, as you'll learn a lot more about the person sharing their good news and strengthen your relationship in the process.

Active constructive response is one of four ways you can respond to people's good news. Before learning how to respond in this way, let's look at how *not* to respond.

- **'Active destructive'** response is when you remove the joy of the reported news by questioning it. For example, on hearing that your gleeful companion has landed themselves a new job: 'But you're already over-stretched. Won't it make you even more tired?' Or: 'Hmmm. I heard they don't pay very well.'
- **'Passive constructive'** response is very common and lacks enthusiasm and support. It's the kind of response you might use when you're too busy to be fully present and are failing to pay attention due to other distractions. For example, you might say, 'Oh, that's nice' as you look at your phone.
- **'Passive destructive'** is the worst kind of response in terms of how it makes the other person feel. It involves completely ignoring the good news and shifting the focus away from the speaker towards yourself, the listener. For example, 'Oh, well I've had some good news too. I'm getting married and I'm moving to Timbuktu.'

The passive responses make the speaker feel unheard, uninteresting and unimportant. They feel invisible, like their news doesn't matter to you at all. This puts up a huge barrier to the warm and enjoyable feelings that good-quality connections generate.

The active responses mean you have listened, but whereas an active destructive response makes the person talking feel deflated, an active constructive response offers enthusiastic support and makes the talker feel heard.

An active constructive response offers enthusiastic support and makes the talker feel heard.

### EXERCISE: Active Constructive Response

The aim is to draw out more information from the person sharing their news and help them to relive their experience and savour the good event. Here's how:

- Use eye contact, smile and nod as they tell you their news.
- Ask active memory questions which appeal to their senses and encourage them to relive the experience. For example, you might say: 'Wow! So how did you feel when she gave you that good news?' Or: 'That's brilliant. What did he say next?' and 'What did you do next?' And: 'When

was this?', or 'You must feel so excited! What about it are you most looking forward to?'
- Tell them you're really happy for them and continue to ask questions.

## 2. Show You Care

Relationships require care and attention in order to develop and deepen the connection between two people. So it's important to be there for people when they need you. Even when people don't ask for your help, just knowing you are there can be support enough.

Giving emotional support to others has actually been shown to support one's own emotional health, even if you're struggling yourself.[2]

### EXERCISE: Actions Speak As Loud As Words
- **Send reminders that you are there and that you care.** From little self-made cards to voice notes or mini-videos sent over the phone, let people know they needn't reply, but that you want them to know you care and that you're available any time should they want to talk about

anything or cry on your shoulder. Offering care and support will mean a great deal.

- **Get the diary out.** Schedule in time to regularly connect with your favourite people so it becomes routine. First consider monthly get-togethers. You could suggest a monthly video call, brunch date or cycling trip to the local pub or cinema on the first weekend of each month. Maybe you could schedule a day trip once a quarter or something seasonal which becomes a tradition – from bluebell walks in spring to a woodland treasure hunt each autumn. Perhaps a bi-monthly laughter date where you watch a comedy series or movie at each other's houses or go see a stand-up comedian.

- **Plan a special day trip.** Pick a close friend or someone you'd like to rekindle your connection with and design a day out with them in mind. Factor in some thoughtful touches based on what they love to do. Perhaps they love rummaging in thrift stores – if so, research a few to visit. If they love to drink tea, treat them to afternoon tea in a local café. Show them you've thought of them and their preferences. According to a Harvard University report on Prosocial Spending and Happiness, those who spend money on other people and experiences are significantly happier than those who spend the money on themselves.[3]

- **Schedule uplifting activities together.** Ask your friends what they liked to do when they were ten years old and whether they'd like to try it again. Is there any way you could enjoy these activities together? It can be a great way to reintroduce your friends to activities which spark joy in them and boost their wellbeing, and you'll create cherished memories too. Perhaps you could attend an evening watercolour class or a roller disco together. Or maybe you could organize a seaside adventure to go rock-pooling or crabbing, if they loved to do that as a child.

Shared social laughter makes us feel more connected to others and even reduces pain.[4]

## 3. Show Your Appreciation

As well as feeling seen and heard, we all like to feel valued. To develop strong bonds with others, it's important to show how much we appreciate them. This doesn't mean feeling obliged to shower people with compliments and praise, but small tokens of gratitude can mean a lot.

To develop strong bonds with others, it's important to show how much we appreciate them.

### EXERCISE: Value Their Value

- **Demonstrate that you see your connections' value.**
  Write a list of words describing the strengths of the
  person you are showing your appreciation for and words
  that come to mind when you think of them. You could
  write the words in calligraphy or paint the words with
  a fine brush. I first did this by writing my daughter's
  signature strengths on a bright piece of yellow card and
  sticking it on her pinboard to serve as a reminder of all
  her wonderful qualities that we value (particularly useful
  for family, as our default may be to nag or moan at them,
  so this provides some balance and reminds them of how
  much you value them too).

- **Let people know you are grateful to have them in
  your life.** Little thank-you cards, notes and letters can
  make someone's day. As can a bunch of flowers or a
  handmade gift. You're not expecting anything in return –
  just letting someone know how much they mean to you.
  And gestures of gratitude needn't cost the earth. Some
  springtimes I spend £10 on ten bunches of daffodils and
  leave them on the doorsteps of people I'm grateful to
  have in my life, with a note of gratitude or encouragement
  telling them how much I value them. It makes the recipient
  feel good and I really enjoy the tradition.

## 4. Show Willing

Sometimes life gets in the way of connecting properly. We might
be too busy with work and family commitments to have the time
or capacity to see friends or we might feel disconnected from

people due to physical or mental health reasons.

When friends don't return calls or messages or forget to get in touch, try to show empathy and understanding. You will likely catch up where you left off when you do get together. Friendships are meant to be devoid of hard feelings, so let any that spring up when a message goes unanswered fall by the wayside and give your friends the benefit of the doubt. People are busy but it doesn't mean they don't care.

That said, if a lack of time is a reason for disconnection, there are ways you can save time and optimize connection in one fell swoop.

---

### EXERCISE: Busy Life Connection Hacks

- **Synergize.** If you have a lot to do, consider ways you could fit multiple tasks into the same time period. List tasks or chores that you need to do each day or week, such as walking the dog, attending an exercise class, food shopping, collecting the children from school, gardening and cooking meals. Consider how you might synergize these tasks with connection. For example, you might need to take some parcels to the post office, walk the dog and have a long-overdue catch-up with a friend. Well, perhaps you could do all three at the same time – invite your friend over for a coffee, then continue your chat as you walk (with the dog) to the post office. Or how about organizing a batch-cooking gathering with a couple of friends, where you share your stove (or theirs) and you each batch cook one dish and share portions with each other. You'll come away with three dishes to pop in your freezer and memories of a good time spent cooking and chatting.

- **Harness technology.** Practice leaving brief voice notes using WhatsApp or sending video messages to friends. We don't always have time to respond to text and WhatsApp messages, to scroll through social media posts or have lengthy catch-up calls over the phone. So, although face-to-face connection is the best way to connect and time should be made to do this, you can always send a video or leave a voice message to let someone know you're thinking of them. Sometimes leaving a voice note updating someone with your news and asking a few questions about their news can be a great way to communicate in an active response way. They can listen intently to your message, note down their own replies and questions and reply via their own voice note. My dear friend Iva and I have been doing this for a while. She lives in Canada while I'm in the UK, and it's a great way to connect deeply with each other in between Skype calls. Vocalizing what you're wrangling with or celebrating without interruption is also incredibly therapeutic. We both feel so much better after recording our own voice notes and hearing each other's.

Pay attention to how using technology to connect makes you feel. If a video call or audio message lifts your spirits, it's worth taking advantage of it. But if you end up with 'Zoom fatique' after one too many online calls, or find yourself feeling self-critical and frustrated as a result of the 'compare and despair' feeling that social media

scrolling can induce, take a break from it. If technology
feels intimidating to you but you can see the benefits, or
if a lack of tech savviness makes you feel even more out
of the loop, look out for internet courses run at your local
community centre or library.

## 5. Learn the Art of Conversation

Conversation doesn't come naturally to everyone and sometimes
we can find ourselves talking about ourselves and what's going
on in our lives without giving other people the chance to speak.
Learning to have more balanced conversations can be a work
in progress.

### EXERCISE: Practice Conversation Starters

Like anything in life, the more we practice something,
the better we get at it, but we may need a little help from
time to time, even when we are talking to people we've
known for ages. Consider the following conversation
starter prompts which you can use to spark meaningful
conversations and deeper connections, rather than chit-
chatting about the weather:

- What's been the highlight of your day/week so far?
- What are you most excited about in your life at the
  moment? What are you really enjoying?

- What are you wrangling with or getting annoyed about at the moment? What are you finding discouraging or challenging?
- Who are you closest to in your family?
- What achievements are you most proud of? Anything we need to raise a glass to?
- How have you been feeling lately? Is there anything you need my help or support with?
- If you could have one superpower, what would that be?
- Who would be your dream dinner party guests and why?
- What is your favourite TV show?
- If you could go anywhere in the world right now (money is no object), where would you go?
- What is your favourite quote?
- What fear would you like to overcome?
- Where would be your dream vacation?
- What kind of music do you listen to?
- What one invention needs to exist?
- What is your biggest accomplishment?
- What's your dream job? (And is it the same as your dream job from childhood?)
- What is your biggest failure/most embarrassing moment? (Be prepared to reveal yours. It is almost impossible to be bored when a person tells you sincerely what they have failed at or what has humiliated them.)

The more you show interest and mutually share with each other, the more you build trust and deepen your connections.

- Strive to balance the conversation by listening more than you talk. It can be easy to ramble, but a monologue is not conversation, so listen, ask questions and avoid interrupting.
- Use names and anecdotes or explanations about how you know the other person when making introductions.
- Learn how to use and read body language, as this contributes to connection more than we realize. For example, the more we mirror the person we're connecting with, the better the connection, as the speaker automatically feels like you are paying attention to them. The more we maintain eye contact, nod and smile, the better the connection and feeling between you too.

## 6. Learn to Be Vulnerable and Cultivate Trust

Working on your ability to trust is not just about how you see others, it's also about giving more of yourself to those you build trust with and practising being more open and vulnerable with them.

There are no guarantees you will never be hurt again by someone else, but the pleasure of deep mutual connection is surely worth the risk. What makes us vulnerable is what makes us beautiful as humans; it is precisely our vulnerability which opens us up to closeness with others, to the reciprocal connection of giving and receiving, which makes connection so worthwhile.

---

*It is precisely our vulnerability which opens us up to closeness with others.*

---

Thankfully, you can learn to build and earn trust, to develop your confidence and self-worth and tweak how you think and behave so you can more readily confide in other people.

Once people have earned your trust, opening up to them will deepen your connection with them. If you close up and avoid sharing your own vulnerability, you stop yourself from being seen. Conversely, when you have the courage to be vulnerable and open, you let yourself be seen, you *allow* people to see you. Until that point, you can't connect as deeply as you deserve to.

*'Courage starts with showing up and letting ourselves be seen.'*
*Brené Brown*

---

**EXERCISE: See the Value in Vulnerability**

- **Choose vulnerability and sharing over guardedness and hiding.** Think about insecurities you might have that you could share. People are often surprised when they get a 'me too!' response. For example, perhaps you struggle with criticism and find you default to defensiveness, and maybe they do too. After discussion you might find this comes down to your mutual desire to feel approved of and fairly evaluated, and it has a lot to do with your shared values of justice and fairness. Or maybe you often feel out of your depth at work and have 'imposter syndrome' where you think you're going to get found out for not being good enough. If you shared that vulnerability with someone, the chances are high that they will have felt the same at some point in their life. If you have insecurities, explain what they are and talk about why you think they might exist. Make any trust issues you have about you rather than them, to avoid a defensive response.

Sharing our vulnerabilities builds bonds because it reveals our human, relatable side and shows we are comfortable enough with someone to let the drawbridge down, to let them in. This leads to the other person doing the same, and soon, in the place of walls, there is only mutual trust.

- **Remind yourself that others may be feeling the same social anxiety as you.** You are not alone in feeling social inhibition. It can feel uncomfortable talking to people when we fear we might say the wrong thing. But if we remember that we all like characters with imperfections, it can remove this fear. And besides, other people are likely just as nervous as you might be. Once you begin to talk to people and invite them to open up, it can be easier to find yourself opening up too. And the more you connect and practice conversing, the easier it becomes.

- **Take tiny steps**. If it feels too daunting to get out into the world to meet new people, set yourself tiny goals you can work towards. For example, you might start by phoning one person each week or joining a small yoga class where you can sit at the back on your mat. Each time you stretch outside of your comfort zone you learn that you can do more than you thought you could. But you can only learn when you dare to try. And your comfort zone naturally expands with experience, along with your abilities. So, each time you try something new or achieve a goal, you'll feel your capabilities growing. Meanwhile, having a focus will give you an anchor to distract you from anxiety.

Up to 70% of people have felt imposter syndrome at some point in their career.[5] (I know I have. Regardless of how many books I've written or how qualified I am or what I've been through and bounced back from in my own life, sometimes I question myself. So here I am being vulnerable. Now it's your turn, because we're in this together.)

## Your Key Takeaways

1. **Listen Well.** The saying 'we have two ears and one mouth for a reason' makes sense when you consider how important listening is to deepening connections. As humans we need to feel heard, and this is only possible when those we're connecting with devote as much time to hearing us as they do to talking to us and vice versa.

2. **Respond Well.** Remember, we all want to feel seen and heard, so when you listen to people and have conversations which make others feel good, you'll develop strong bonds. So listen intently, ask active memory questions and think about how you make other people feel in your response to what they have to say.

3. **Show You Care.** Taking time to reach out to let people know you care is a golden opportunity to deepen your connection and show your support, as is demonstrating your commitment to your connections by organizing experiences you know they will delight in.

4. **Show Your Appreciation.** Demonstrate your joy at having the people you cherish most in your life by expressing your gratitude in various ways and showing how well you know them by explaining what it is about them that makes you feel so grateful. This will make the person you're connecting with feel good and, because gratitude is a positive emotion in itself, will make you feel good too. In this way, letting people know they matter also benefits us. A win-win.

5. **Show Willing.** Taking responsibility for your relationships is important in order to sustain and maintain them. It's important to take the initiative and find the right balance between accepting and empathizing with the busy-ness of other people's lives and showing your willingness to organize and arrange

opportunities to connect which can be synergized around tasks on your to-do list.

6. **Learn the Art of Conversation.** Whether you are a strong communicator or struggle to interact socially, it's useful to practice and be prepared by taking prompts with you when you meet up with others, so you can to kick-start the conversation. Once the conversation is in flow, and there are fewer awkward silences, it becomes easier to relax and connect.

7. **Learn to be Vulnerable and Cultivate Trust.** Blame and shame can make us all feel bad but, when we share how we feel with others, we often find we have more in common that we think. What's more, having the courage to share our vulnerabilities with others encourages them to do the same with us, removing barriers to connection and opening us up to each other. This builds trust.

Once you have optimized your connection skills, boosted your confidence as a result and know how to develop your relationships and make the most of them, you can focus on finding and maintaining the right kind of relationships to help bring the best out of you and those you connect with.

# CHAPTER 6

# GET BETTER CONNECTIONS

*'I've always felt that when you do feel loneliness, it's always
a kind of inverse measure of what you actually belong to. It
actually tells you where to go.'*
David Whyte

The level of support we gain from our relationships has been
shown to influence our level of life satisfaction and wellbeing.

A 75-year-long Harvard study of 724 adult men found that not
only do 'good relationships keep us happier and healthier', but,
more specifically, our brains function better, nervous systems
relax and emotional pain is reduced when we have someone
we can rely on in our lives.[1]

Psychologists have found that, to keep loneliness at bay, we
need, at the very least, one or two meaningful relationships.[2] We
need to be able to confide.

However, all connections are not created equal.

Rather than the quantity of connections you have, it's the *quality* of those relationships that counts. So, it's not just connection with other people which keeps loneliness at bay – it's connection with the right kind of people for *you*.

This explains why you need not be physically alone to feel lonely. If you're surrounded by the wrong people for you, and have a high quantity of low-quality connections, you may feel desperately lonely.

This is why psychologists say that tools to help lift people out of loneliness aren't just about helping people to meet more people and forge new networks; they're about forging networks that are *meaningful*.

So, how can you gauge the calibre of a connection?

This generally comes down to how visible and valuable you feel and how mutually supported you are.

Connection is all about *feeling*.

The deeper the sense of belonging you feel, the better the quality of the connection; the more visible and valuable and supported you *feel*, the better the quality of connection. Hence the importance of learning how to connect as best you can, as covered in the preceding chapter.

The deeper the sense of belonging you feel, the better the quality of the connection; the more visible and valuable and supported you *feel*, the better the quality of connection.

How other people make you *feel*, therefore, is at the very heart of any relationship. That's at the core, the crux of all connection.

> '*People will forget what you said, people will forget what you did, but people will never forget how you made them feel.*'
> Maya Angelou

So, the quality of connection can be determined by:

- How other people make you feel about yourself
- How other people make you feel about the world around you
- How other people make you feel about your relationship with them

This is why it's so important to do the work to connect with yourself, as it helps you define with more clarity who you are and, therefore, who the kind of people are that you are most likely to foster good-quality relationships with; the kind of people who will make you *feel good*.

And once you've learned how to connect better with others (Chapter 5), you can work on getting better connections – both by developing existing connections and finding new ones. To do that you can:

1. Understand the difference between types of connection
2. Connect with the right people for you
3. Understand patterns of behaviour and response
4. Meet new people and create interaction opportunities
5. Ask for help
6. Volunteer your help
7. Connect through kindness

## Understand the Difference Between Types of Connection

Your connections needn't be like you to be liked by you. They may be very different to you and have different backgrounds or views yet still light you up when you are in their company.

Similarly, how aligned you are with others in terms of your/ their values, interests and strengths doesn't necessarily correlate with how close you are to them. However, the better people make you feel and the more you feel you can trust them, the closer you can choose to become. Before you can assess which relationships to devote more time to developing, it's important to understand the different types of connection, how they impact loneliness and which types need the most attention.

### Types of Connection

As we touched on at the start of this book, there are three main types of connection (inner, middle and outer circle), which correspond with the three types of loneliness: emotional (intimate), social (relational) and existential (collective) (as defined on page 7).

### 1. Inner Circle

Close confidantes with whom we share deep bonds of trust and mutual support make up our more intimate inner circle. According to Professor John Cacioppo in his book *Loneliness: Human Nature and the Need for Social Connection*, his studies on the causes and effects of loneliness carried out at the University of Chicago reveal the importance of having at least one person we can count on to call in the middle of the night for support should we need it. Having such a connection with one or two people buffers against mental illness and bolsters mental wellness. According to Professor Cacioppo, having at least one close friendship, plus a relationship network of five or more key 'confidant(e)s', means we are less likely to be lonely and more likely to describe ourselves as 'very happy'.[3]

This inner core of supportive relationships can include romantic partners, and always includes your closest friends and perhaps family members you can rely on during times of crisis, such as parents, grandparents or siblings. These people are the ones you *choose* to spend time with often and have the deepest connection with – the relationships you cherish the most.

You may have initially developed these close friendships as a result of connecting as soon as you met as children at school, or at college or university; you may have become firm friends because you attend the same church or your children attend(ed) the same toddler group or school. You might have met each other while going through a similar life experience, be that giving birth or recovering from an illness, and you may share a sense of humour and/or have similar goals. You may have chosen to develop these relationships because you can confide in these people, they show an interest, listen, encourage and appreciate you. These are the connections to prioritize.

## 2. Middle Circle

Our middle circle consists of 15 or more casual friendships or family relationships with people we may see regularly who belong to the same social circle as us. Experts call this social network our relational 'sympathy group', which might include people who make us laugh and whom we feel we can talk to, but whom we don't tend to know on a deeper level. So, you might share the same sense of humour and have things in common, but you're not as close with these people as you are with your inner circle. The more often you see friends in this group and the higher the quality of connection in terms of alignment and how they make you feel, the less lonely you are likely to be.

## Outer Circle

Our outer circle consists of weaker ties we may have with people who belong to the same group, neighbourhood, school, team or nationality as us. Being part of this collective wider group of acquaintances gives us our sense of social identity and makes us feel like we belong somewhere. Rather than count these people as 'friends', these neighbours, colleagues, team and group community members are people whom we don't know much about at all, except perhaps their name, occupation and maybe where they live. We might talk about the weather and less meaningful topics, but it can still be comforting to have some interaction with this outer circle.

This outer circle might include people you may have known since school but still keep in touch with via social media. They often arise out of groups of people you join because of shared interests in creative arts or sports, or they may be members of the team you volunteer with.

As mentioned at the start of this book, each type of connection provides a defence against their corresponding type of loneliness, so the type of loneliness you are experiencing will dictate which type of connection you may wish to focus on the most.

For example, if you feel that you have a lack of people in which to confide (emotional loneliness), you should focus on developing more intimate inner-circle connections. If you have someone to confide in but don't feel like you have a particularly supportive social network, your relational middle circle could do with some attention. Whereas if you have plenty of 'connections', yet feel detached from them all, it's worth working on your collective outer circle – to find people you have something in common with, no matter how loosely, that can foster a spark of belonging (perhaps by joining an online group of new parents in your local area or pet owners who have the same breed of dog or a local book club or sports team). If you experience all three types of loneliness, then while you can work on fostering all three types of connection, you should prioritize the first.

To gain even more clarity, spend some time working out who fits in which circle and which circles need to be worked on the most.

### EXERCISE: Circle Time

- In the centre of a blank piece of paper, draw round the top of a cup to create a circle. Inside, write down the names of up to six people who are in your inner circle: those you confide in, rely on and would choose to spend time with over anyone else.

- Next draw round a breakfast bowl to create a middle circle. Write down the names of 1–15 people with whom you talk to regularly and have things in common, but have a more casual connection.

- Draw round a larger mixing bowl to create your outer circle and jot down the names of neighbours, colleagues and team members who you know well enough to speak to but not well enough to refer to as 'friends'. You might not ordinarily consider these people as important, but completing this exercise may illustrate that a smile or a wave to or from a neighbour matters more than you'd previously appreciated.

- Think about your relationship with each of these people and mark each one out of ten in terms of how good each person makes you feel.

- Change pen colour. Next to each name, write down what you get from each relationship. For example: love, support, laughter, fun, encouragement, interest, advice, knowledge and so on.
- Is there any scope for movement between circles? For example, are there any acquaintances in your middle or outer circles who make you feel really good and who you'd like to get to know better? Equally, is there anyone in your inner or middle circle who makes you feel bad, whom it might be in your best interests to see less of?
- Write down any actions you can take as a result of doing this exercise that would help you get to know certain people better or improve your relationship.

This exercise will help you assess whether you have the right blend of connections you need to protect you from loneliness, i.e. some inner circle, middle circle and outer circle connections, to protect you from emotional, social and collective loneliness. The next step is to assess whether the relationships you already have are good enough quality to devote energy to and maintain.

### Connect with the Right People For You

Having already done the work to better connect with yourself, before going out to establish *new* connections it makes sense to examine your *existing* relationships to ensure you have the right connections for you.

As such, you need to check the relationship balance in your 'social account' just like you check your financial balance in your bank account. Your 'social account' is essentially the level of good-quality, healthy connections you currently have.

Each time you take action to develop existing relationships or add new quality connections or remove a toxic or draining relationship from your account, your social account balance increases and your susceptibility to loneliness decreases. Ultimately, the more you invest in the right relationships for you, the healthier your social account balance.

The more you invest in the right relationships for you, the healthier your social account balance.

### EXERCISE: Audit Your Relationship Quality

While loyalty and history can be important, when it comes to keeping loneliness at bay, they are not as important credentials as wellbeing and how people make you feel. Relationships can either bring us great joy, fun and support, or they can bring us sadness, frustration and discouragement. They can heal our hearts or break them. They can energize us or drain us.

So it's worth spending some time evaluating existing relationships and considering how people make us feel.

- Look at each name in your inner and middle circles. Answer the following questions by writing the names of those connections who fit these criteria either on a piece of paper or in this book . You may find the same person is more than one of these things. Or you may struggle to find names to fill these roles – that's okay, because over the following pages you'll read about ways to meet new people or heal relationships with others who may come to fill them.

- ° Who energizes you and is the person you would describe as your 'ray of sunshine'?
- ° Who is your cheerleader and encourager?
- ° Who is your most trusted confidant(e)?
- ° Who is your rock and defender who'll always be there for you and fight your corner?
- ° Who is your entertainer?
- ° With whom are you most able to be yourself, to be authentic? (This is worth evaluating because when we have to cover up our true selves and put on a performance in order to fit in, this creates counterfeit connections which lack authenticity and depth.)
- ° Who listens to you most and shows a real interest?

- Have another look at your inner and middle circles and consider the following questions:

  - ° Does anyone deplete your energy?
  - ° Does anyone repeatedly judge or bully you?
  - ° Does anyone wind you up or press your buttons?

The names on this second list could either be moved from your social circle completely or be considered as relationships to heal or work on (see the 'Gain Deeper Understanding of Others' Behaviour and Your Reactions' exercise on page 125).

- Next, answer the following questions for each person in your inner circle and middle circle. Do they:

  ◦ Show an interest and listen to you?
  ◦ Do their best to understand you?
  ◦ Make you feel held, supported and appreciated?
  ◦ Enable you to turn to them during tough times?
  ◦ Encourage you and celebrate your wins with you?
  ◦ Share your values?
  ◦ Make you laugh often?
  ◦ Make you feel like you belong?

If you can say yes to at least five of these questions, they are most likely a good-quality connection.

If you can say yes to the first four, they are *most certainly* a good-quality connection.

But what if someone doesn't pass your relationship audit?

## Understand Patterns of Behaviour and Response

Before you go cutting people from your life, it's important to consider your answers in more detail, because they may have more to do with you and your own experiences, insecurities and beliefs than your connections' actions.

For example, did you answer 'no' to whether they 'make you feel like you belong' because they make you feel left out/like you're not good enough? If so, this may have more to do with your own insecurities about fitting in and differing values than how they behave. For example, they might take pride in their home and appearance, which might make you question whether you have made enough of an effort, or they might be a high achiever, which might also make you feel comparatively bad, even though you have admirable qualities in your own right. They might be super health-conscious, which again might make you feel like you don't measure up. But these feelings aren't down to them unless they pointedly make snide remarks about you. The point is we are all different; even friends who share a sense of kinship have different values, lifestyles and priorities. Not sharing these doesn't mean we don't belong, as long as we see, hear and value each other.

As such, before cutting old friends out of your life, consider whether the relationship is worth saving and working on. Sometimes by working on relationships to heal old wounds and considering our patterns of response, we can create stronger existing relationships and learn how best to enter into stronger new ones too.

So, just as it's important to find the right balance between looking inward and looking outward when evaluating and validating *ourselves*, it's equally important to find this same balance when evaluating and validating our relationships. On the one hand, you need to consider how different people make you feel and consequently which connections deserve to be invested in. On the other hand, you also need to consider your own role in those relationships and whether your own triggers and patterns of response might require some attention.

---

**EXERCISE: Gain Deeper Understanding of Others' Behaviour and Your Reactions**

Old wounds, the way we've been brought up by our parents and subsequent patterns of response can disrupt existing and future connections. You may 'armour up' and push people away by default in certain situations or you may be triggered to overreact in others.

These negative interactions may cause you to view someone as a negative connection and consider moving away from a relationship with them. However, before you do this too quickly, it's worth reflecting on your own personal triggers and consider with compassion why others might behave in the way they do. Developing your understanding about why we each behave the way we do can be the gateway to stronger and better relationships.

- **Consider your default responses to other people.**
  First, choose a family member, spouse or friend with whom you sometimes struggle to get along or whom you find yourself judging negatively. For example, perhaps this person makes remarks which make you feel bad, so you judge them for being unkind and, as a result, may keep them at arm's length. Or perhaps you find yourself flaring up when this family member doesn't consider

your opinion. Maybe it's the regular criticism and lack of encouragement from your spouse that bothers you.

- **Reflect with compassion about why they might behave in this way and/or why you respond in this way.**
  Consider their/your values and how those values may impact behaviour. Perhaps you have strong values about fairness and justice, which makes you default to defensiveness when you feel an accusatory tone is being used. Perhaps they put everyone else first so struggle when their help isn't needed. Maybe you strongly value integrity, so can't deal with any dishonesty or sneaky behaviour. Maybe they are a perfectionist, so expect the same from others.

- For example, what if the person who makes negative remarks behaves in this way because they've been hurt in the past and they lash out as a defence mechanism? What if their remarks are a way to get your attention and solicit a response, as they are keen to befriend you, but struggle to know how?
  Maybe you flare up when your family member doesn't consider your opinion because it triggers a memory of a past pain when you were ignored as a child. But perhaps, when you explore this, you realize they often do ask for your input, except when they know you're busy (so they have your best interests at heart). And maybe they don't realize how much this matters to you or where this reaction stems from?
  Perhaps the lack of encouragement and overt criticism from your spouse bothers you because your

parents were so encouraging that you miss that and consequently struggle with criticism. But what if your spouse's parents rarely gave them encouragement or praise, so this wasn't modelled for them? And what if their upbringing instilled in them such a desire to please their parents that as a result they became a perfectionist with incredibly high expectations, which they now expect of you?

- **Decide on an action that would help reduce your own negative response, demonstrate understanding and improve your relationship.**
For example, what if you gave the person who makes negative remarks a chance, were warmer towards them and ignored their critical banter? Perhaps your warmth might melt their negativity and help them open up to you. Maybe you'd see another side to them and you'd enjoy their company rather than avoid it. Or, if not, at least you'd know you tried.

Perhaps explaining to your partner why you react in this way when you feel like you're being ignored would help heal that wound and give them a deeper understanding of your needs while helping you avoid overreacting as often in future.

You might decide to let it go when your perfectionist spouse points out what you're doing wrong without praising what you're doing right, to accept their suggestions more readily as helpful ways to improve and get the encouragement you seek from other friends who find it easier to offer that to you (and decide to reward and encourage yourself too).

This kind of examination of other peoples' behaviour and our own reactions to it can lead us to let go of old wounds and move forward in a more accepting and compassionate way. When we consider different ways of looking at things and think about other people's points of view and how their own life experiences may have impacted those, we can gain a deeper understanding of our own default responses and why we both react in certain ways.

Once you've audited your existing relationships in this way, you'll be fully prepared to maintain the right ones for you and go out into the world to find the right kind of new relationships for you too; to cultivate new, quality connections.

It's time to get proactive.

Developing your understanding about why we each behave the way we do can be the gateway to stronger and better relationships.

## Meet New People and Create Interaction Opportunities

The idea of meeting people may feel daunting at first, which is why you've (hopefully) done the groundwork in boosting your self-confidence and getting to feel more comfortable in your own skin, but it's better to try meeting new people than not bother trying. The former gives you a chance to make new connections; the latter guarantees you staying stuck where you are.

There are many ways to meet new people, no matter whether you live in a busy city or rural village. Joining a group is perhaps the most obvious way to meet potential new friends. The reason many types of therapy often include support groups is because being part of a group has been shown to repair emotional damage and reduce stress. It also provides the opportunity for synchronicity as people share and listen, talk and respond, tell stories and relate to those stories with their own tales. The way groups interact is therapeutic and supportive.

We've been gathering together in groups since the dawn of time, when we got together around campfires. Group gatherings provide a natural way of connecting with each other, so whether it's a book club, art group, support group or choir, joining a group of people with shared interests can be a wonderful way to lift yourself out of loneliness, because everyone is there for the same reason.

While there is less openness in our middle-circle connections, a welcoming smile and sense of familiarity and recognition is enough to spark a sense of belonging in us. And sometimes connections made in a group setting can become close friends and move into that trusted inner circle.

## EXERCISE: Commit to Joining In

- Take up a new hobby or pursue an old one. Enrol in a class to learn more about something you've never tried. Whether it's cooking, pottery, photography or hiking, joining a class has the double benefit of learning how to improve your skills doing something you enjoy with like-minded people.

- Join a group specific to a type of situational loneliness. For example, if you are feeling lonely as a new parent, a local 'mum and tots' group could help. Joining a bereavement charity support group could help if you are lonely as a result of losing a loved one, while joining University of the Third Age (U3A) – a network of learning groups aimed at encouraging older people to share knowledge, skills and interests, could help if retirement has left you feeling bereft of social contact and lacking of something to do.

- Look online or in your local newspaper for a local choir, singing group or dance classes, then commit to going along to try it out. You've got so much more to gain than to lose in doing so. According to research, singing groups can generate the most satisfying social bonds because of the 'ice breaker effect' of singing together. Dancing in pairs is another great way to break down social barriers. Coordinated movements and shared interests help people develop connections, plus endorphins are released when we sing and dance, so the feel-good factor is practically guaranteed.

## Get Online

Plenty of blame is heaped on technology for increasing levels of loneliness, but, when used in a balanced way, it can still be useful in lifting us out of loneliness, especially when we're socially isolated. As people across the world discovered during the Covid-19 pandemic, being able to connect virtually via apps like Zoom, WhatsApp and Houseparty enabled virtual connection during a time when we were unable to physically connect with others during lockdown. Many people have met their partners via online dating apps. And social media can be a wonderful way to connect with like-minded communities and groups of people who share the same interests as you, or to connect with people who live locally. If you struggle with social anxiety, joining online groups and interacting with people from the safety of your own home can be a great way to meet new people, gain confidence and forge new relationships before meeting up in person.

---

### EXERCISE: Cultivate Online Connections

- Decide on what you'd like to gain from connecting virtually. Do you want to find love? Find people who enjoy the same hobbies as you? Or find local parents who you could potentially meet up with once you've started to cultivate a friendship online?

- To find local connections, look for local groups on Facebook or try Nextdoor.co.uk, which connects members of local communities across Britain.

- To connect with people who share the same interests as you, use search engines to find online groups with members who share your interests. Create a profile and introduce yourself. Or join the group and participate by commenting on existing posts and gradually get to know people that way.

- Use technology to augment rather than replace real life face-to-face connection.

- Monitor mobile device usage and put your phone away to stay present and maintain balance between looking up (connecting) and looking down (disconnecting).
- See past the illusion of social media to avoid 'compare and despair' and remind yourself that the frequently filtered posts do not reflect reality so there's no point comparing your blooper reel with everyone else's highlights reel.

## Get Offline

While new technologies have improved convenience and made a lot of tasks easier, they have in some ways removed the opportunity for us to connect directly with people.

These days we can do our shopping online, which can be delivered without any human interaction. And even when we do shop in a physical store, we can self-checkout without interacting with anyone. Work can be done from home and we can go to the gym or swimming pool without as much as a smile to those exercising alongside us.

But we *can* build connections back into our daily lives if we choose activities which provide us with the opportunity to interact.

### EXERCISE: Cultivate Face-To-Face Interaction

Brainstorm interaction opportunities you'd feel comfortable with to add to this list. For example, you could:

- Shop locally and regularly in the same place and use a till manned by staff rather than a self-checkout.
- Get a pet. As well as providing companionship to ease loneliness, owning a pet provides the perfect opportunity to meet fellow pet owners and, if it's a pet you can walk, gets you out and about.
- Create routines. As well as providing the comfort of certainty, walking regularly in your local park or outside space gives you the opportunity to meet others who are routinely going about their day. Regularly seeing the same faces and waving to neighbours can help us feel connected to a community.
- Write down some of your own ideas that will get you out and about and create opportunities to interact with others.

## Ask For Help

In addition to group support, there is a range of support for anyone experiencing loneliness, including:

- Social groups focused on shared interest
- Lunch clubs
- One-to-one befriending schemes

There are also a range of foundation services which come before these initiatives and provide ways to rekindle existing relationships by provision of transport, technology and guidance on how to use it.

Additionally there are approaches which aim to create the right environment for loneliness to be reduced. These are called 'structural enablers', and they try to develop new structures within neighbourhood communities, such as community allotments and positive ageing initiatives which show later life as a time of opportunity, from Dementia Friendly Communities and University of the Third Age to Age Friendly Cities.

Meanwhile, community allotments have been created by Connecting Communities projects across the UK and beyond, bringing people in the community together for a shared purpose. And, if you don't drive or feel uncomfortable going to a club alone, volunteers are often available to drive people to lunch clubs, while some providers bring community street parties to you, so you can meet your neighbours and establish or reinforce community relationships. You can get involved and find your local loneliness service by visiting: www.redcross.org.uk/get-help/get-help-with-loneliness/find-your-local-loneliness-service. See also the Useful Resources section at the back of this book for more information and global resources.

There's help for different ages, too. Marmalade Trust organizes Christmas Day Parties for older people who would otherwise be spending the day alone, along with a telephone befriending service; Mush is a free app set up by two lonely mums who met in a rainy playground and decided to create an app to help mums make friends with other local mums in their area, similar to The Motherload, which was set up to help new mothers combat loneliness. 'In Good Company' offers intergenerational projects which bring together younger and older people to share digital skills.

From Mental Health Mates, which 'helps you find your we, because you are not alone', to Casserole Club, which enables volunteers to share extra portions of their own home-cooked food with people in their area who aren't always able to cook for themselves and/or may be feeling lonely, there are a great many 'connection clubs' available for those experiencing loneliness to join. Find a MeetUp group and attend one near you. These are for people of all ages who move to new areas and want to find new friends.

It can be difficult for people to tell when we're feeling lonely or depressed or anxious. They are, in this way, invisible. It's not that people don't care; it's that people will be unlikely to know how you're feeling. So do ask for and accept help. You are not being a burden (that's just one of those old inaccurate thoughts); these initiatives have been set up especially to help people in your situation.

### EXERCISE: How to Ask For Help

- Identify who you have to talk to: are there any family, friends, neighbours or work colleagues you could get in touch with? Make sure you have their landline, mobile phone numbers and email addresses (sometimes, as a first port of call, it can be easier to reach out via email or text message than talking to someone directly, so it's useful to have every option).
- Call your GP to arrange an appointment if you are feeling lonely and feel like you have nobody to turn to. They can and will help as the government has now rolled out 'social prescribing' across England as part of the National Health Service's frontline duty of care. Social prescribing is a way that anyone can now access a range of amazing wellbeing interventions, which they may not have known

about or had access to before. You don't need to visit your GP specifically about how you feel, whether you are feeling lonely, depressed or anxious. But, if you do, they can help. What's more, you might visit your doctor with a physical complaint and, during your appointment, it may become clear that isolation is causing you problems. Now, rather than just offer medication, the doctor will refer you to a link worker whose purpose is to treat loneliness, depression or anxiety and who will create a tailored plan to suit your specific wellbeing needs. This could involve connecting you with an art or adventure therapy group, a nature walk initiative or even a surfing initiative, along with housing, debt or employment advice.

- Turn to the 'Useful Resources' section at the back of this book and explore the wide variety of helplines and services aimed at targeting loneliness.

## Volunteer Your Help

As well as asking for help, one of the most fruitful ways of getting help is to give it. Some initiatives are doing wonders to create virtuous circles of volunteering, where service users can become volunteers. So you can use a service yourself, then volunteer to help others who need it. Some employers even pay staff for days they can volunteer for other organizations as part of their Corporate Social Responsibility initiatives.

Volunteering can be a wonderful way to meet new people and feel part of a community working together for a good cause. Other benefits of volunteering come from the good feelings which being of service gives us. Helping others has been proven to boost wellbeing levels and improve mental health.

Serving others quite literally serves us too.

So, not only does voluntary work help others, it helps the volunteer. Serving others quite literally serves us too. Here's why. The positive impact is two-fold. Volunteering makes the volunteer feel good because:

1. The act of service is meaningful and provides a sense of purpose.
2. Acts of kindness create positive emotion and provide what's known as 'giver's glow'.

So, with one action, volunteers can tick off two out of six of the pillars of wellbeing that positive psychologists have defined as the ingredients for flourishing, for optimal human functioning.

Professor Martin Seligman, one of the founders of the field of positive psychology, developed five measurable pillars of psychological well-being[4] under the acronym PERMA, each of which contribute to optimal human functioning and flourishing. A sixth pillar was added more recently when the link between mind and body became more apparent, so Vitality was added, making the acronym – PERMA-V. These six pillars of wellbeing include:

1. Positive emotion
2. Engagement

3. Supportive relationships
4. Meaning
5. Achievement
6. Vitality

And, given that volunteering often requires you to work within a team and focus on engaging tasks towards shared goals, voluntary work can tick off even more of these 'pillars of wellbeing', including 'engagement', 'supportive relationships' and 'achievement'. And, if the voluntary work includes being active, (for example taking people on country walks or any other form of exercise), that would be a full house of flourishing ingredients, with 'vitality' ticked off the list too.

The two primary feel-good factors involved in volunteering, however, are the positive emotion that comes from being of service and the meaning which comes from doing purposeful work.

As Viktor Frankl says in *Man's Search For Meaning*, which he wrote following his eventual release from Auschwitz, having a purpose gives life enough meaning and hope to withstand adversity. Having worked as a psychiatrist before the war, Frankl noticed how it was the men who comforted others and gave away their last piece of bread who survived the longest – these observations offered proof that everything can be taken away from us except the ability to choose our attitude in any given set of circumstances and to find meaning and purpose, using it to help us survive and thrive.[5]

Terry Waite, whose purpose of being a father and humanitarian work kept him going during his five years alone in captivity, says that 'when you are giving away of yourself, in actual fact, you are giving *to* yourself at the same time; you're doing yourself good.'

## EXERCISE: Give Help

- Refer to your answers about what causes you care most about, what your skills and talents are and what you enjoy doing, and use these answers to help you decide which kind of charity or initiative you'd most like to volunteer your time to help.

- Conduct some internet research to find a list of charities or local initiatives. If you don't have internet access yourself, you can get help with your research at your local library.

- Visit the websites of those you've selected and email or phone them. Most charities have a section answering questions about what kind of volunteers they are seeking, the duties they undertake and the process of applying to volunteer.

## Connect Through Kindness

*'The best way to cheer yourself up is to try to cheer somebody else up.'*
*Mark Twain*

Just as the benefits of volunteering are mutual, so are small everyday acts of kindness, from checking on a neighbour or handing out bunches of daffodils to people who look like they might need cheering up, to simply offering a smile. All of these acts of kindness give us a sense of purpose and make us feel stronger and more connected.

So whatever we spend on being kind – be it time, money, energy or effort – we also receive back, via boosted positive emotions, a greater sense of meaning and improved social connection. This is what the Buddhist monk Matthieu Ricard calls 'psychological economics'. In terms of wellbeing, both giver and recipient win.

Also, sometimes loneliness is made harder not because you feel like you have nobody to share your burdens with, but because you only have your own burdens to bear. It's a natural human instinct for us to want to help other humans, so intentionally being kind offers relief from having only our own problems to deal with.

Kind acts activate the reward centre in our brain (our 'nucleus accumbens', as it's known). In a study by University of Oregon researchers, the pleasure/reward centres in people's brains lit up and released endorphins (hormones that reduce pain, relax us or make us feel happy) during voluntary charitable giving, providing evidence of the 'warm glow' that we feel.[6] This explains why performing, or even thinking about performing, acts of kindness produces a tangible high. Furthermore, kindness fosters togetherness and cooperation.

All this means that we are literally wired to feel good about doing something that aids the survival of the human race.

According to various scientists, such as Martin Seligman and E. Diener in their 2002 *Psychological Science* study on very happy people, performing acts of kindness boosts our wellbeing more than any other exercise tested.[7]

What's more, kindness can positively impact our sense of belonging too. Through generosity without expectation, altruism can help us root ourselves in our community. We are more likely to become a valued member of our community when we are kind to those within it.

---

### EXERCISE: Commit to Being Kinder

- Bundle kind acts together into a morning, afternoon or full day of kind acts, rather than sprinkling them across a week. Psychologists have found that setting aside 'kindness mornings' or devoting days to altruistic acts has an even greater impact on our wellbeing than individual random acts here and there.

- Make newcomers to your community feel welcome and find ways to help those who've lived in your neighbourhood for a long time feel a part of the community. You could pop a welcome card through the letterbox of people moving in, including a self-drawn map of places of interest, or you could organize an American supper for neighbours, where each person brings a dish of their own to create an instant dinner party.

- Experiment. Write a list of possible random acts of kindness and set a small budget. For example, you could buy small bunches of flowers, make some bookmarks and gather a handful of pound coins, then, on a day when you're feeling low, go out and tape pound coins to parking meters, pop bookmarks with positive messages into library books and hand bunches of flowers to busy mums pushing pushchairs or people who look like they could do with some kindness. Some days you might plan kind acts, such as mailing a package to a sibling or friend who's currently having a stressful time at work. Other days they might happen spontaneously. For example, you might decide to buy a coffee for the people behind you in the queue or give up your seat on the bus for a mother with toddlers in tow. Be on the lookout for ways to make peoples' days better and enjoy the giver's glow. As Aesop (of Fables fame) said, 'No act of kindness, no matter how small, is ever wasted.'

Just knowing there is someone out there who cares is a great comfort in itself, even if that person is a kind stranger. What's more, when it comes to taking action to lift ourselves out of loneliness, we can benefit greatly from attending clubs and getting involved with our local communities, but we can also benefit when we are alone just from knowing those other people are there. That knowledge helps us turn the pain of loneliness into the solace of solitude when we're alone and makes all the difference as you step into a new life, free from loneliness.

## Your Key Takeaways

1. **Understand the Difference Between Types of Connection.**
   Not all relationships are equal. They can vary in quality and
   depth of connection depending on how often we see people,
   how aligned we feel to them and, most importantly, how they
   make us feel. But rather than devote all of our attention to only
   our closest friends and ignore everyone else, it's important to
   have people in our inner circle, middle circle and outer circle as
   each type of connection combats a different type of loneliness
   and, together, gives us a greater sense of belonging.

2. **Connect with the Right People For You.** The better you know
   yourself the more authentic relationships you can develop with
   people you feel the deepest sense of kinship with. They may
   have wildly different personalities to you, different strengths
   to you and come from a different background. They may even
   have different opinions to you but, if you share similar values,
   like doing similar things and make each other feel good, there's
   a good chance your relationship will stand the test of time.

3. **Understand Patterns of Behaviour and Response.** Conflict
   can come and go in relationships and it doesn't make us feel
   good, but it doesn't mean we should give up or walk out on
   relationships which can also offer support and nurture us in
   other ways. If we can move past righteousness and our quest
   for 'rightness' in relationships, and be curious enough to
   question our own responses and consider other points of view,
   we can create harmonious connections, heal past wounds and
   deepen existing relationships.

4. **Meet New People and Create Interaction Opportunities.**
   When it comes to connecting, we can't wait around for people
   to come to us. Rather, it's important to be proactive and
   create interaction opportunities by finding groups of people

and individuals with whom we can build on mutual affinities and interests, and by maximizing the chance to interact when we're out and about by acting intentionally. There are also a number of initiatives and community projects that have been established to help connect local groups of people with shared interests. The key is to commit to joining in.

5. **Ask For Help.** When you ask for help you are giving someone the opportunity to make a difference and feel good, because that's how helping you will make them feel. It will also make you feel better because a problem shared really is a problem halved. It's important to ask for help, especially now that social prescribing means you can be prescribed with numerous wellbeing interventions to help you make the most of life.

6. **Volunteer Your Help.** Serving others makes us feel good because it reminds us of our value, it gives us a sense of purpose and it also gives us an opportunity for human connection, which enables us to strengthen our social bonds. It feels good to be of service to others.

7. **Connect Through Kindness.** Supportive relationships are about give and take. And being supportive is at least as beneficial to our wellbeing as being supported. Sometimes service serves us even more than those we serve. As well as giving us 'givers' glow', performing acts of kindness can root us in our community to give us a sense of belonging.

# CONCLUSION

# FINDING BALANCE

*'A season of loneliness and isolation is when the caterpillar gets
its wings. Remember that next time you feel alone.'*
Mandy Hale

Too much of one thing is never good for us – whether that's
chocolate, alcohol, cheese or time in constant company or time
in solitude. Too much time in solitary confinement can lead to
psychological and physiological issues in prisoners. But being
constantly surrounded by others without any time alone can also
be detrimental.

Just as we need social connections and supportive relationships
to function well and live good lives, it's also important for our
emotional welfare to be able to enjoy the time and space to pause
and be alone.

We need a balance of both social activity and the soothing
solace of solitude.

Babies demonstrate this beautifully. As babies, we completely rely
on our caregivers to feed, carry and change us. Yet studies reveal
that babies also turn away from parents from time to time, not just
to sleep but to follow the inbuilt requirement to disengage too.

As adults we rely on others, such as farmers and utility
companies, to provide us with food to eat and running water to

drink, even if we don't come into contact with those providers. Humans are interdependent. And supportive relationships have been found to be one of the most important predictors of longevity and wellbeing in life. Yet our wellbeing also benefits from periods alone, especially if we spend our days working with others. We need time alone to rest, recuperate and process.

In other studies, teenagers who balance social time with solitude are well adjusted and enjoy their social interactions more if they've had the opportunity to spend some time alone first.

And while our culture of busy-ness and the need for constant productivity can prevent us from turning inward, finding the right balance between external and internal demands, between noise and peace, between social time and alone time, is critical.

I hope this book enables you to find the right balance between connection and solitude, between interaction and isolation, and that you are able to take one tiny step followed by the next tiny step towards feeling more connected.

Our social circles, no matter how big or small, can satisfy our human need for connection, but I hope that you now also feel equipped with the resources to better connect with yourself, to give yourself the encouragement, support and compassion that the best kind of connections offer. I hope this book has also provided you with an idea about what social support would give you – such as guidance, encouragement and reassurance – along with some tools to help you to cultivate a positive social circle and make progress towards lifting you and anyone you know out of loneliness.

Unlike Terry Waite, who spent five whole years in isolation, we have the freedom to go out, connect and learn. We may be isolated or lonely – perhaps a disability is preventing us from having the freedom to venture out much – but we are not imprisoned like Terry was. We can ask for help and receive it;

we can take small steps to better connect with ourselves and with others, to find the solace and the pleasure in solitude and connection alike.

I hope this book helps you to navigate your way out of loneliness, by identifying it, managing it and finding the support you need – but also by helping you to shift how you view time alone, connect with yourself better and build your resilience so you can cope better whenever you feel lonely.

I hope you've discovered some ways to cultivate a positive social circle of your own, to lift yourself out of loneliness and to lift others out of loneliness too. Because we're in this together, and together we rise.

# ACKNOWLEDGEMENTS

Gratitude to my dearest James and Brooke for your love and support.

To Tanis Frame for connecting me with your Decide To Thrive tribe of such remarkable and wonderful women and for (along with the amazing Amy Kubanek) enabling me to connect deeper to myself.

To all of my D2T soul sisters and to those friends who see, hear and encourage me and allow me to see, hear and encourage them.

Thank you all.

# ENDNOTES

## Introduction

[1] Loneliness New Zealand. *Welcome to Loneliness NZ*. Available from: https://loneliness.org.nz

[2] Australian Psychological Society and Swinburne University (2018). *Australian Loneliness Report*. psychweek.org.au/wp/wp-content/uploads/2018/11/Psychology-Week-2018-Australian-Loneliness-Report.pdf

[3] Loneliness New Zealand. *Welcome to Loneliness NZ*. Available from: https://loneliness.org.nz

[4] G. Sundström, E. Fransson, B. Malmberg and A. Davey (2009). 'Loneliness among older Europeans', *European Journal of Ageing*, Vol. 6, No. 4, p. 267.
N. Savikko, P. Routasalo, R.S. Tilvis, T.E. Strandberg and K.H. Pitkälä (2005). 'Predictors and subjective causes of loneliness in an aged population', *Archives of Gerontology and Geriatrics*, Vol. 41, No. 3, pp. 223-33.

[5] Sense (2017). *Someone cares if I'm not there*. Available from: https://www.sense.org.uk/support-us/campaigns/loneliness

[6] Age UK. *No-one should have no-one*. Available from: www.ageuk.org.uk/get-involved/no-one
Relationships Australia (2018). *Annual National Survey*. Available from: www.relationships.org.au/about%20us/annual-reports/relationships-australia-annual-report-2018

[7] S. T. Child and L. Lawton (2019). 'Loneliness and social isolation among young and late middle-aged adults: Associations of personal networks and social participation', *Aging and Mental Health*, Vol. 23, No. 2, pp. 196-204.

[8] Loneliness New Zealand. *Welcome to Loneliness NZ*. Available from: https://loneliness.org.nz

[9] T. Henderson (2014). 'Growing Number of People Living Solo Can Pose Challenges', *Stateline, Pew Charitable Trust*. Available from: www.pewtrusts.org/en/research-and-analysis/blogs/stateline/2014/09/11/growing-number-of-people-living-solo-can-pose-challenges

## Chapter 1

[1] D. Perlman and L.A. Peplau (1981). 'Toward a social psychology of loneliness', *Personal Relationships*, Vol. 3, pp. 31-56.

[2] L.C. Hawkley, M.W. Browne, J.T. Cacioppo (2005). 'How can I connect with thee? Let me count the ways', *Psychol Sci,* Vol. 16, No. 10, pp. 798-804.

[3] Viceland UK Census Survey (2016). 'What Vice Readers Fear the Most'. Available from: www.vice.com/en_uk/article/nnyk37/what-vice-readers-fear-the-most-hannah-ewens-love-loneliness

[4] Timothy D. Wilson *et al* (2014). 'Just think: The challenges of the disengaged mind', *Science*, Vol. 345, No. 6192, pp. 75-7.

[5] D. D. Russell, L. A. Peplau and M.L. Ferguson (1978). 'Developing a measure of loneliness', *Journal of Personality Assessment,* Vol. 42, No. 3, pp. 290-4.

[6] J. Bowlby (1969). *Attachment. Attachment and loss,* Vol. 1. New York: Basic Books.

J. Bowlby (1980). *Loss: Sadness & depression. Attachment and loss,* Vol. 3 (International psycho-analytical library No. 109). Hogarth Press.

[7] R. Nowland, E.A. Necka and J.T. Cacioppo (2017). 'Loneliness and Social Internet Use: Pathways to Reconnection in a Digital World?', *Perspectives on Psychological Science*, Vol. 13, No. 1, pp.70-87.

[8] I. Pantic (2014). 'Online Social Networking and Mental Health', *Cyberpsychol Behavioral Society Network*, Vol. 17. No. 10.

[9] B.A. Primack *et al* (2017). 'Social Media Use and Perceived Social Isolation Among Young Adults in the U.S.', *American Journal of Preventive Medicine*, Vol. 53, No. 1.

[10] Ibid.

[11] Ibid.

## Chapter 2

[1] Campaign to End Loneliness. Available from: www.campaigntoendloneliness.org

## Chapter 3

[1] A. Koller (1991). *Stations of Solitude*. Bantam Books.

[2] W. Duan, S.M.Y. HoXiaoqing Tang, T. Li and Y. Zhang (2014). '*Character Strength-Based Intervention to Promote Satisfaction with Life in the Chinese University*', Journal of Happiness Studies, Vol. 15, No. 6, pp. 1347-61.

[3] W.H. Frey II (1985). *Crying: The Mystery of Tears*. Winston Press.

[4] J. Beadle *et al* (2012). 'Trait Empathy as a Predictor of Individual Differences in Perceived Loneliness', *Psychology Rep*, Vol. 110, No. 1.

[5] M. Csikszentmihalyi (2008). *Flow: The Psychology of Optimal Experience*. HarperCollins.

## Chapter 4

[1] H. S. Friedman and L. R. Martin (2012). *The Longevity Project: Surprising Discoveries for Health and Long Life*. Plume.

[2] C. H. Cooley and H. J. Schubert (1998). *On Self and Social Organization*. University of Chicago Press.

[3] R. Hanson (2014). *Hardwiring happiness: The practical science of reshaping your brain – and your life*. Rider.

[4] R. W. Levenson *et al* (1993). 'Long-Term Marriage: Age, Gender, and Satisfaction', *Psychology and Aging*, American Psychological Association, Vol. 8, No.2, pp. 301-13.

[5] B. Fredrickson (2011). *Positivity: Groundbreaking Research to Release Your Inner Optimist and Thrive*. Oneworld Publications.

[6] T. Waite (2017). *Solitude*: Memories, People, Places. SPCK Publishing.

## Chapter 5

[1] S. L. Gable, G. C. Gonzaga, and A. Strachman (2006). 'Will You Be There for Me When Things Go Right?', *Journal of Personality and Social Psychology*, American Psychological Association, University of California, Vol. 91, No. 5, pp. 904-17.

[2] O. S. Curry, L. A. Rowland, C. J. Van Lissa, S. Zlotowitz, J. McAlaney, and H. Whitehouse (2018). *'Happy to help? A systematic review and meta-analysis of the effects of performing acts of kindness on the well-being of the actor'*, Journal of Experimental Social Psychology, Vol. 76, pp. 320-9.

[3] E. W. Dunn, L. B. Aknin, M. I. Norton (2013). 'Prosocial Spending and Happiness: Using Money to Benefit Others Pays Off', *Current Directions in Psychological Science*, Vol. 23, No. 1.

[4] R. Dunbar, R. Baron, A. Frangou and E. Pearce (2011). 'Social laughter is correlated with an elevated pain threshold', *Royal Society of London, Series B: Biological Sciences*, Vol. 279, pp. 1161-7.

[5] J. Sakulku, J. Alexander (2011). 'The Impostor Phenomenon', *Behavioural Science Research Institute, International Journal of Behavioural Science,* Vol. 6, No. 1, pp. 75–97.

## Chapter 6
[1] Harvard Medical School (2014). *Harvard Study of Adult Development*. Available from: www.adultdevelopmentstudy.org
[2] L.C. Hawkley *et al* (2008). 'From Social Structural Factors to Perceptions of Relationship Quality and Loneliness: The Chicago Health, Aging, and Social Relations Study', *The Journals of Gerontology: Series B,* Vol. 63, No. 6.
[3] Ibid.
[4] W. T. Harbaugh *et al* (2007). 'Neural Responses to Taxation and Voluntary Giving Reveal Motives for Charitable Donations', *Science*, Vol. 316, p. 1622.
[5] V. Frankl (2004). *Man's Search For Meaning*. Rider.
[6] W. T. Harbaugh *et al* (2007). 'Neural Responses to Taxation and Voluntary Giving Reveal Motives for Charitable Donations', *Science*, Vol. 316, p. 1622.
[7] E. Diener and M. E. P. Seligman (2002). 'Flourish: A Visionary New Understanding of Happiness and Wellbeing', *Psychological Science,* Vol. 13, pp. 80-3.

# USEFUL RESOURCES

**Loneliness Helplines and Services**

**Red Cross and Co-op's Connecting Communities scheme**
www.redcross.org.uk/get-help/get-help-with-loneliness

**The Samaritans**
www.samaritans.org
Call free on 116 123

**The Silver Linex**
www.thesilverline.org.uk
A free, 24-hour, confidential helpline for older people age 55+.
Call free on 0800 4 70 80 90

**The Mix**
www.themix.org.uk
Provides confidential help for under 25s
Call free on 0808 808 4494
Text THEMIX to 85258
Use the online chat service

**Campaign to End Loneliness**
www.campaigntoendloneliness.org
The Campaign to End Loneliness believes nobody should be lonely in older age.

## Let's Talk Loneliness

www.letstalkloneliness.co.uk

Tips, advice, local support, toolkit and resources.

## MeetUp

www.meetup.com

Sign up to find meet ups in your local area. Most events/activities are either free or low cost.

## Nextdoor

www.nextdoor.co.uk

Find people in your local community.

## UK Social

www.uksocial.wordpress.com

The place to make new friends, activities across the UK.

## Reengage

www.reengage.org.uk

Call companions support older people who live alone.

## Age UK

www.ageuk.org.uk/services/befriending-services/

Call 0800 678 1602

Befriending service to beat loneliness in later life

## Eden Project Communities

www.edenprojectcommunities.com

Bringing communities together and inspiring them to make positive changes where they live.

## Sense

www.sense.org.uk

A national disability charity that supports people with complex communication needs to be understood, connected and valued.

## Mind

www.mind.org.uk

A mental health charity

## Social Anxiety

www.social-anxiety.org.uk

A volunteer-led organization providing news, advice, meetings, chatroom, forums, support/social groups and info on cognitive behavioural therapy.

## The Lonely Hour

www.thelonelyhour.com

A podcast in which people open up about their struggles with loneliness and isolation.

## Dementia Friendly Communities

www.alzheimers.org.uk/get-involved/dementia-friendly-communities

## University of the Third Age

www.u3a.org.uk

## The Marmalade Trust

www.marmaladetrust.org

A charity dedicated to raising awareness of loneliness and helping people make new friendships. Organizes Christmas

Cheer events for those who would otherwise be spending the day alone along with a telephone befriending service.

## National Alliance on Mental Health
www.nami.org/Support-Education/Mental-Health-Education
Works to improve the lives of Americans affected by mental illness.

## Mush
www.letsmush.com
A free app connecting mums with other mums nearby, set up by two lonely mums who met in a rainy playground.

## The Motherload
www.the-motherload.co.uk/blogzine/molo-community/
Set up to help new mothers combat loneliness.

## In Good Company
www.norfolk.gov.uk/what-we-do-and-how-we-work/campaigns/in-good-company
Offers intergenerational projects which bring together younger and older people to share digital skills.

## Mental Health Mates
www.mentalhealthmates.co.uk
Helps you find your we, because you are not alone.

## Casserole Club
www.casseroleclub.com
www.casseroleclub.com.au

Casserole Club volunteers share extra portions of home-cooked food with people in their area who aren't always able to cook for themselves.

## The Cares Family
www.thecaresfamily.org.uk/3g-social-clubs
Helps three generations of people find connection and community in a disconnected age via social clubs.

## Ladies Circle
www.ladiescircle.co.uk
For women between ages of 18 and 45 to make new friends, have fun, fundraise for local charities.

## Tangent
www.tangent-clubs.org
For women aged over 45 with a focus on making friends, enjoying a programme of interesting and fun activities.

## Men's Sheds Association
www.menssheds.org.uk
0300 772 9626
Community spaces for men to connect, converse and create to help reduce loneliness and isolation.

## Spice
www.spiceuk.com
Adventure group for ordinary people who want to do extraordinary things.

**Explorers Connect**
www.explorersconnect.com
Helping people to live more adventurously.

**Friends For Good - Australia**
https://friendsforgood.org.au/
Australian Loneliness Charity.

**Loneliness.org.nz**
https://loneliness.org.nz/
Conquering loneliness in New Zealand.

**NZ Coalition to end loneliness**
http://sewn.org.nz/a/osMRUVv

**Super Seniors NZ**
www.superseniors.msd.govt.nz/

**The Selwyn Foundation**
www.selwynfoundation.org.nz/charity/social-isolation-loneliness/
Creating places for New Zealanders to meet up and connect

**Friends of the Elderly, Ireland**
https://friendsoftheelderly.ie/what-we-do/friendly-call-service/

**No Isolation**
www.noisolation.com
One-button computer for those with no experience using
smartphones or computers to send or receive messages and
photos, and conduct video calls. Available in eight European
countries.

**The Loneliness Project**

thelonelinessproject.org

The Loneliness Project in Canada is a collection of personal stories about loneliness.

**Friendly Phone programme – Canada**

www.redcross.ca/how-we-help/community-health-services-in-canada/saskatchewan-friendly-phone-program

**Seniors Centre Without Walls – Canada**

www.edmontonsouthsidepcn.ca/classes-health-resources/seniors-centre-without-walls/

**Good Samaritan**

Mobile phone application where volunteers can sign up to deliver food and medicines, drive patients to appointments and phone socially isolated individuals.

**Beyond Differences**

www.beyonddifferences.org

US-based organization helping young people tackle social isolation at school.

**Online communities**

For parents: www.mumsnet.com

For grandparents: www.gransnet.com

For over 18s: www.elefriends.org.uk

For carers: www.carersuk.org/forum

For over 55s: www.thesilverline.org.uk

### Social Prescribing
Find out more at: www.england.nhs.uk/personalisedcare/social-prescribing/

## Volunteering

### British Volunteering Portal
www.do-it.org

### V-Inspired
www.vinspired.com
Site for young people aged 16–25 who wish to do voluntary work.

### Volunteer Match
www.volunteermatch.org
Puts volunteers together with causes they care about in their own neighbourhoods.

### Volunteer
www.volunteer.gov/s
America's Natural and Cultural Resources Volunteer Portal.

### Go Volunteer
www.govolunteer.com.au
A portal run by Volunteering Australia to match volunteers with opportunities.

### Volunteer World
www.volunteerworld.com
Volunteer abroad

**European Voluntary Service**
www.europa.eu/youth/EU/voluntary-activities/european-
voluntary-service_en

**International Volunteer HQ**
www.volunteerhq.org/gb/

**Student Volunteer Army New Zealand**
https://sva.org.nz/

## Resources to Help with Meditation

### Insight Timer Meditation app
www.insighttimer.com
Free library of more than 60k guided meditations.

### Headspace
www.headspace.com
Help with meditation, mindfulness and sleep.

## TriggerHub.org is one of the most elite and scientifically proven forms of mental health intervention

Trigger Publishing is the leading independent mental health and wellbeing publisher in the UK and US. Clinical and scientific research conducted by assistant professor Dr Kristin Kosyluk and her highly acclaimed team in the Department of Mental Health Law & Policy at the University of South Florida (USF), as well as complementary research by her peers across the US, has independently verified the power of lived experience as a core component in achieving mental health prosperity. Specifically, the lived experiences contained within our bibliotherapeutic books are intrinsic elements in reducing stigma, making those with poor mental health feel less alone, providing the privacy they need to heal, ensuring they know the essential steps to kick-start their own journeys to recovery, and providing hope and inspiration when they need it most.

Delivered through TriggerHub, our unique online portal and accompanying smartphone app, we make our library of bibliotherapeutic titles and other vital resources accessible to individuals and organizations anywhere, at any time and with complete privacy, a crucial element of recovery. As such, TriggerHub is the primary recommendation across the UK and US for the delivery of lived experiences.

At Trigger Publishing and TriggerHub, we proudly lead the way in making the unseen become seen. We are dedicated to humanizing mental health, breaking stigma and challenging outdated societal values to create real action and impact. Find out more about our world-leading work with lived experience and bibliotherapy via triggerhub. org, or by joining us on:

🐦 @triggerhub_

🅕 @triggerhub.org

📷 @triggerhub_